SAINTS PRESERVED

AN A-Z OF SOUTHAMPTON FC

BY NICK ILLINGSWORTH

First Published in 2007
by Elephant Books
c/o **4 Newgate Court, Paradise St,**
Coventry, CV1 2RU

Thanks

Karen Phillips and Harvard for patience and encouragement , Lorna Illingsworth for sometimes indulging me and pretending she supports Saints, Kev McMahon for hours of brainstorming, Chris Newman for help and encouragement, Hagiology Publishing without whose books I would have had to spend a lot more time on research, Ian Murray, Dave King and Jez Gale at The Daily Echo, Graham Hiley, David Luker and Andy Oldknow at the Football Club for help and allowing me access, James and Richard Jablonski & Derek Long and anyone else who has had to put up with watching a game with me over the years, members of **www.theuglyinside.net** message board for reminding me that football can never be as important as listing your top 3 crisps, Graham Smith & Neville Hadsley for turning a dream into reality but most especially to the Supporters of this great Club for making it what it is, if there is anyone else I have forgotten then please accept this as a personal thank you and oh yes and in the great tradition of Thank You's, anyone else that knows me !!!

About The Author

Nick Illingsworth started following Saints in the 1971/72 season aged 10 and has barely missed a home match since then, starting his Dell career sitting on the wall separating the west stand terraces with the Archers Road end and ending it 29 years later sitting on the very same wall, in a happy state of inebriation after the Farewell Dinner on the Dell Pitch in the summer of 2001.

Educated at Redbridge School followed by short career's in both Shipping and Office Equipment, he was a co founder of The Ugly Inside fanzine in April 1988 and editor of **www.theuglyinside.net**, a founding member of both the Southampton Independent Supporters Association and The Saints Trust he has also been a regular contributor to The Daily Echo on all subject's Saints .

He has worked for the past two decades as a Financial Advisor and has a 12 year old daughter Lorna.

He lists his favourite player as Matthew Le Tissier, his favourite goal as Le God's final Dell goal against Arsenal and his favourite game as the 1976 FA Cup Final, he can usually be found on match days in The Kingsland Stand bemoaning the manager's selections, the boards incompetence, the price of his half time pint and the woeful inadequacies of the Club's scouting system in the Seventies that failed to spot his talent on Green Park in Millbrook.

Front Cover Clockwise from top left: Derek Reeves, George O'Brien, Terry Paine, Mick Channon, Charlie Wayman, Ted Bates (R) and Lawrie McMenemy (L), Ron Davies, Francis Benali. Centre: 1976 FA Cup winning squad.

Foreword

On 15th January 1972 I stepped inside The Dell for the first time ever and so began a love affair that so far has lasted over 35 years, spanning something approaching 1,500 games and, in monetary terms, must have cost me a small fortune. But I'm not out of the ordinary.

I, like millions of others, not just in Southampton, but across the country, indeed the world just love my football team and I'm sure that by reading this, you do too.

"By far the greatest team the World has ever seen" is a chant often heard in British football, and Saints can't claim to be as universally known as some, but that's perhaps what makes us proud of our team and that is what bonds Saints supporters together in a way that Man Utd, Chelsea and Arsenal fans can never experience.

In the main, we don't choose to be Saints supporters; we are born to it and that's what makes it so special. If you are abroad and you see a Saints shirt you stop and talk to the wearer, you know you have common ground, you know that you wont be talking to someone whose only connection with the area is Sky TV.

Over the years I have made many friends in football. I still see faces I can remember from that first season on the Milton Road End. I also see those that are more recent converts to the cause, that doesn't make them any less of a fan that me, it just makes them younger. Sadly for them they missed what up to this point has

been the golden period in Saints history, the Cup win of 76, the Keegan years and of course latterly the genius that was Matthew Le Tissier.

So that brings me to why I have written this volume. For many years there has been a drastic shortage of books on Southampton Football Club. What has been written has been excellent; however I have always felt that what has been missing, has been something that brings the Club to life for the average fan, tells the facts and sifts out the fiction, records those great times for posterity and makes us all remember why we love the game and those great moments that made our hair stand on end, whether it be for you, Charlie Wayman, promotion in 1966, Wembley 76, Kevin Keegan signing, maybe Cardiff in 2003 or perhaps for some it was the sheer joy of those last day escapes from relegation.

Sadly at the moment, it's not a great period for the club. However sometimes you need to experience a few bad times in order to cherish the good times when they return. Perhaps this book will bring back a few memories and tell you a little bit about Southampton FC that you didn't know, and all with a little bit of humour.

If it does, then all the fun I have had researching it has all been worthwhile, it's been 35 years in the making, hopefully volume two wont be another 35.

Nick Illingsworth

A
Abandoned Games

Perhaps the most high profile Southampton game to be abandoned, was in October 1983 when the pitch at Filbert Street for the game against Leicester City was more suited to water polo than football. Possibly because the Match of the Day cameras were there, the referee decided to start the game and hope the pitch would dry off. But more rain made the game a farce. Although it provided much hilarity for the rest of the season, whenever clips were shown, the game was finally abandoned scoreless, on 22 minutes.

Some would say this had a greater impact on that season than was realised at the time. When the fixture was re-arranged a month later, Leicester scored, ironically in the same minute the first game had been abandoned and Saints were beaten 2-1. The final league table would see Saints finish the season runners up to Liverpool, the gap between the clubs being three points.

John McGrath

In February 1977, Saints travelled to promotion chasers Nottingham Forest and lead 1-0 with a first-minute goal from Nick Holmes. With Saints well in command over an out of sorts Forest side, the fog started to come in from the River Trent forcing the referee to abandon the game early in the second half. The replayed game saw Forest cruise to a two goal lead before Saints pulled one back. Forest held out for the win and gained promotion by a one point margin over Bolton Wanderers.

Ale House Brawlers

When Saints beat Liverpool at the Dell in September 1970, the visitors' manager Bill Shankly felt so strongly about Saints tactics, he accused them of playing "Ale house football." His accusation wasn't completely without foundation. Ted Bates had realised that skill alone wouldn't be good enough to keep his side in the top flight and had blended the skill of Channon and Davies with the muscle of McGrath and Hollywood to name but two. It wouldn't be the last time that Saints would be accused of being "Ale House Brawlers." In honour of that title we give you our top ten of those Saints players that you would want alongside you if you were meeting Vinnie Jones or Roy Keane on a dark night.

Goalkeeper
John Burridge
Put bluntly John "Budgie" Burridge was several sandwiches short of a picnic and didn't hesitate to stick his head in where it hurt. To hone his reactions, he famously used to sit on his sofa with his gloves on when he was watching TV and get his wife to throw a ball at him from all angles.

The garage at his old home in Chilworth allegedly still has the dents in it from where he would throw himself onto the tarmac drive after saving the rebounds.

Full Backs
Ivan Golac
Ivan wasn't perhaps known for his desire to hurt an opponent, merely for the fact that he never shunned a tackle and never seemed to come off worse in one.

Dennis Hollywood
The hardman's hardman. Ask any member of the Saints side from the late 1960s or early 70s who they think the hardest man in the side was. They would tell you that you definitely saw stars if you were tackled by Hollywood. It's a testament to his ferociousness that he stands out in this side, in a position that's blessed with men of iron. In 1971 Hollywood got a seven-week suspension from the F.A. Sadly it wasn't to be a record, as you will find by reading on.

Centre-Halves

John McGrath

Known to all and sundry as "Big Jake." In his five-year stay he was described by manager Ted Bates as "like a barn door, but slightly more mobile." He was the foundation of an X-rated back four that should have seen under-15s refused admission to watch them.

Cliff Huxford

Having played his last game for the Saints in 1966, memories of Huxford should have dimmed, but not for the older Saints fans. They'll tell you that a head-to-head between Huxford and Hollywood would have filled the Dell alone. Luckily they were on the same team. The Saints players of that era swear that none was harder than Cliff and that none have been since.

Midfield

Brian O'Neill

"Buddha" as he was known, had four years at the club, during which time he never owned a pair of his own boots. Even more remarkably he never wore a pair of shin pads. O'Neill made it his personal mission to look after Mick Channon on the pitch, earning him his fair share of attention from referees. If Dennis Hollywood thought that he was hitting the record books with a seven-week ban from the FA, he got a surprise, when O'Neill copped nine weeks, a record for English football at the time.

Jimmy Case

Jimmy had a reputation long before he arrived at the Dell and whilst playing for Southampton he certainly did nothing to diminish it. Hard as nails, he was frightened of no one, but he could also play a bit as well. He joined

Brian O'Neill

Saints as he was about to turn 31 and was still a regular in the side seven years later. Nevertheless, Saints fans feel he was released prematurely by Ian Branfoot, to allow the new manager to demonstrate who was boss.

Terry Hurlock

He didn't play many games for Saints but he certainly imposed himself in those he did. Looking somewhat like a gypsy, with his long curly hair and earring, he had an aura off the pitch to match. Those who met him found he was just as terrifying as his displays on the field suggested.

Barry Horne

Perhaps the surprise choice in this side. Barry Horne had been to university and was seen as a bit of an academic, but his tackling on the pitch was frankly, uneducated. Not a hard man in the conventional sense, he was more the thinking man's assassin. His legendary tussles with Stuart Pearce were eye-watering affairs.

Horne refused to back down and never showed when he was hurt. He was perhaps the only player that Pearce truly respected, at least judging by the way the Forest man made it his personal mission to take lumps out of Horne whenever they met.

Forwards

Joe Jordan

Coming to the Saints at the end of his career, he didn't enjoy the best of times, but he had lost none of his bravery. Jordan was legendary for his toothless grin, but what many didn't know was that he had lost those teeth on the Dell pitch whilst playing for Leeds in Ted Bates' testimonial match. Whether he came back to try and find them is unclear.

Alan Shearer
Making his debut as a teenager, Shearer soon started to earn his reputation as a player who flinched from no one at the Dell. Indeed he and Neil Ruddock were known as the "Bruise Brothers" by the fans who recognised their tenacity and determination to give as much as they took.

Substitutes
Mark Dennis
In any other club's greatest hardmen list, "Psycho," as he was christened, would have walked into the team, and probably been made captain as well. Unfortunately or perhaps fortunately, the other teams didn't have Dennis Hollywood. Whilst at the Dell, though, Mark Dennis became a cult hero. Some would say he wasn't that hard and that's what made it more frightening. He was fearless and had no more care for his own safety than that of his opponents. Dennis was cursed with getting the red mist so often, he was sent off for offences far less serious than those that had not been spotted by the ref.

Francis Benali
Like Mark Dennis, Franny finds himself on the bench due to his playing in a position that is choc-a-bloc with hardmen. But make no bones about it, Franny could dish it out and take it with the best of them. He was versatile as well, and was able to play in midfield in a scenario best described as "have studs will travel."

Uli Van Gobbel
He only played 34 times for the club, but he made Mike Tyson look timid and used this to good effect. If he'd stayed longer, he certainly had the potential to become a first choice in this side.

American Football
Believe it or not, The Dell played host to American Football. In the First World War the ground was used for a match between two US Army teams. Southampton Mayor Sir Sidney Kimber, ceremoniously kicked-off the game.

A few decades later an American Army side, stationed in the City during the latter part of the Second World War, played several "home" games under the name of "14th Port." A programme exists for a game between 14th Port and US Engineers dated 29th October 1944, kicking off at 2pm at "The Dell Field."

The games were watched by US servicemen based in the area, augmented by bemused locals. The Echo reported that "It was very unlike the football of these islands." They did not confirm whether the crowd indulged in Budweiser and foot longs.

The Antelope Ground

Antelope Ground
The Antelope Ground was on the corner of St Mary's Road and Brintons Terrace next to the Royal South Hants Hospital. Up until 1885 it had been the home of the Hampshire County Cricket Club prior to their move to the County Ground in Northlands Road. Southampton F.C. moved in and made steady progress.

A record attendance of 12,000 gathered in 1895/96 for the visit of Sheffield Wednesday in the FA Cup, prompting the Club to consider purchasing the ground. However, no agreement could be reached with the ground's owners and it was sold for development. It left Saints homeless in the summer of 1896.

Appearances

Top Five Record Appearances (substitute in brackets)
League, FA Cup, League Cup, Europe Only

	League	Cup	Total
Terry Paine	709 (4)	96 (0)	805 (4)
Mick Channon	507 (3)	84 (2)	591 (5)
Nick Holmes	437 (7)	95 (0)	532 (7)
Tommy Traynor	434 (0)	47 (0)	481 (0)
Matthew Le Tissier	377 (66)	74 (11)	451 (77)
Jason Dodd	372 (27)	77 (3)	449 (30)

Attendances

Highest Attendances at The Dell

Div 1.	31,044	v. Manchester United. 1969/70
Div 2.	30,586	v. West Bromwich Albion. 1948/49
Div 3.	25,042	v. Reading. 1959/60

Lowest Attendances At The Dell

Div 1/Premier	9,028	v. Ipswich Town. 1993/94
Div 2.	1,875	v. Port Vale. 1935/36
Div 3.	5,721	v. Newport County. 1956/57

Record Attendance at St Mary's
32,151 v. Arsenal. 2003/04

The highest attendance for any Southampton fixture remains the 100,000 who packed into Wembley on May 1 1976 for the FA Cup Final a figure unlikely to be surpassed.

Awards

Kevin Keegan	1982 PFA Player of the Year
Steve Moran	1982 PFA Young Player of the Year
Matthew Le Tissier	1990 PFA Young Player of the Year
Peter Shilton	1990 PFA Merit Award
David Jones	1998 LMA Manager of the Year
Lawrie McMenemy	MBE

B

Ted Bates

Ted Bates unarguably did as much for Saints as Bill Shankly did for Liverpool. It is no overstatement to say that Ted was the man who built the foundations of the modern club.

Ted Bates joined Saints in 1937 aged 19. Initially known as Eddie to his family, he soon became Ted to all in Southampton. Unfortunately his career was interrupted by the war. He served in the Army, although he still played for the club throughout the duration. It meant that although his playing career spanned 15 years, his official appearance total was only 216 games. It's said that everyone has 15 minutes of fame and Ted certainly had more than that, but he also had 15 minutes in goal. In January 1951, he deputised whilst keeper Hugh Kelly had to go off for treatment.

After Ted retired from playing in 1953, the club slipped down into the Third Division South. Many older Saints supporters claim the two events are not unconnected. He became reserve team coach, then first team manager. He held the job from 1955 till 1973. After

Ted Bates (right) with Lawrie McMenemy

handing over the reigns to Lawrie McMenemy, he then served the club as Chief Executive for five years, Director for a further 15 and finally as President from 1998 until his death on 28th November 2003. Ted Bates' unbroken service had lasted over 66 years.

During his time as manager, Bates took the club from the Third Division (S) up to the top flight for the first time ever, where he kept them till his retirement. He also oversaw an FA Cup semi final in 1963, as well as the club's first forays into European competition.

Although there are other candidates for the title of Mr. Southampton, perhaps none can match Ted. He had the title more formally bestowed upon him in 2001, when he was made a Freeman of the City. Ted had been awarded an MBE earlier that year. It was only fitting that he had the honour of ceremoniously locking the gates at the Dell for the last time in 2001. It was equally appropriate that he cut the ribbon at the opening of the new St Mary's stadium, the same year.

Saints fan and author David Bull penned a fitting tribute to Ted with his biography *Dell Diamond* published to mark Ted's 60th anniversary at the Club in 1998. It was a measure of his popularity that many of his old colleagues assembled for a dinner in his honour. A modest man, he would have enjoyed the camaraderie, but hated the fuss.

Sadly an attempt by supporters to honour the great man by erecting a statue outside St. Mary's went tragically wrong in March 2007. The sculptor got the dimensions inexplicably wrong, leaving a memorial that looked more like an effigy of comedian Jimmy Krankie than a fitting tribute to one of the club's greats.

The offending edifice was taken down within days and club Director Leon Crouch commissioned a replacement out of his own pocket. Suffice to say, the supporters of Southampton Football Club know the debt they owe to him, statue or no statue.
1937-53. 216 apps. 64 goals. Manager, 1955-73.

Francis Benali

Francis Benali was one of the most popular players to pull on a Saints shirt, even if at times he wasn't always appreciated by his own supporters. Franny, a local lad, made his debut in October 1988, playing his final game in February 2003 in the Cup run of that season.

In those 15 seasons he played 341games for the club, scoring only one goal. However, there are many who would say that it was the most memorable scored at The Dell.

Francis Benali

It came in December 1997 against Leicester City. By then Franny's lack of finding the net had become legendary. Strangely, he had been a prolific scorer as a forward in the youth team, but he hadn't looked like breaking his duck in almost a decade. Then came the magic moment.

A Matt Le Tissier free kick found an unmarked Benali who buried a bullet header in the net. It was perhaps the only goal in Saints history to be greeted by silence, initially at least. Benali, who admitted afterwards that he had a goal celebration well rehearsed for a number of years, forgot his own script and just ran around like a mad man. Saints fans went wild, many of whom still boast, "I was there when Franny scored."

Benali's testimonial in May 1997 was more pantomime than game of football and a capacity crowd roared with laughter as the current Saints side took on an "Ex-II" including then England Internationals and former Saints, Alan Shearer and Tim Flowers. No one can remember the score, although the local paper had it at 15-15.

Since leaving the club, Francis has played for local club Eastleigh in the Conference South, as well as having stints coaching at St Mary's. Benali also co-owned a curry house in the City, Kuti's, where the "Benali Biriani" is the signature dish. Francis Benali is surely one of the nicest men to have played professional football.
1988-2003. 341 (48) Apps. 1 goal.

Mel Blyth: FA Cup Hero
Mel Blyth was already 30 when he joined Saints in September 1974 from Crystal Palace, for a £60,000 fee. It seemed to Saints fans, disgruntled from their relegation from the top flight the previous season, that Lawrie McMenemy was signing a few old crocks.

Mel Blyth

Fortunately they were soon proved wrong. In his first season, Mel became player of the year. His second would be his peak, as he was the perfect foil to the bluster of Jim Steele in the centre of defence. Blyth was a virtual ever-present in his three seasons with Southampton. The arrival of Chris Nicholl heralded his departure, at the age of 33. After leaving the Dell, Mel finished his league career at Millwall. He now lives in Surrey and is a director of a building firm. 136 apps. 7 goals.

Brazil
"It's just like watching Brazil" is an oft-sung terrace anthem, but do Brazilians sing "It's just like watching Southampton?" If they don't, they should do, because the birth of the game in Brazil stems directly from Southampton.

In 1894, 19-year-old Charles Miller stepped of a ship in the port of Santos (co-incidentally the Portuguese for Saints). After spending 10 years being educated in England, Miller had in his possession a pair of football boots and two balls.

Miller had attended Bannisters school in Southampton and played for Southampton St Mary's and London amateurs, Corinthians, prior to his departure. It was at the Antelope ground he learnt the game. His first team opportunities were limited, but he was to return to Brazil with a great enthusiasm. "What have you got there?" asked his Father, as he stepped off the ship. "My degree," replied his son.

Charles' expatriate father worked for a railway construction project in Sao Paolo, and the son was now returning to the country of his birth. Miller was surprised to find that no one there knew anything about the game of football.
If Brazilians didn't know how to play the game, Miller decided, he would teach them. Soon he had marked out a pitch, recruited enough interested people to form two sides and after explaining the rules, the first ever game of football was played in Brazil. Within fifteen years football was the biggest sport in Brazil.

Miller is even now, remembered in Brazil. His trick of flicking the ball up with his heel is still used and referred to as a "Charleira" or "Charles," and Central Sao Paulo has a street, Praca Charles Miller.

Teams from both Southampton and Corinthians travelled to Brazil to played against São Paulo Athletic Club and other teams in São Paulo. After a tour by Corinthians to Brazil in 1910, a new team was formed. Following Charles Miller's suggestion, they took the name of Corinthians. In 1948 Saints were invited to tour Brazil.

They made the long sea journey to South America on

the SS Andes. During their month-long tour of the country, they played eight games against the cream of Brazilian football, winning twice, drawing one game and losing five. However, the statistics don't reflect the competitive nature of the games. Saints only real crushing defeat being in the opener against Fluminese.

It's hard to gauge today the true debt Brazil owes Southampton Football Club. If Charles Miller had never enjoyed the game of football as much as he did whilst in Southampton, then Brazil just might not have dominated the World Football scene as they have.

Craig David, before he was famous, in the white coat in the crowd at The Dell. This picture was used in The Echo for a Face in the Crowd picture in 1999 and David was selected as the winner of a Saints shirt

C
Celebrity Fans

Southampton is a long way from the Kings Road, so unfortunately can't match the likes of Chelsea for star-spotting in the crowd. However there are a few well-known supporters to look out for:

Fiona Phillips
Anchorwoman of GMTV for the last decade, although better known to the class of '77 at Millbrook school for bunking-off and going to Anderlecht to watch the Cup Winners Cup.

Will Champion
A rabid Saints fan when not drumming for Coldplay and having tea with Chris and Gwyneth Paltrow. He's one celebrity that hasn't forgotten his roots and retains his season ticket in the Kingsland Stand. Allegedly

Coldplay's breakthrough hit "Yellow" was about the 1976 FA Cup Final, or possibly not.

Craig David
Brought up on the Holyrood Estate, there are many who say that Craig was a boyhood Chelsea fan. However, his Saints credentials were confirmed when the local paper revealed he'd been picked out of the crowd, pre-fame, at a game against Everton in 1999 to win a team shirt. David has appeared on stage wearing a Saints shirt from time to time.

Pete Devereux
One-time half of the Artful Dodger UK Garage chart act and record producer. Also credited with discovering Craig David.

Chris Packham
Wildlife expert and broadcaster, Chris was brought up in the Bitterne Park area of the City and is a lifelong Saints fan and season ticket holder.

Centenary

Southampton's first official game was on 21st November, 1885 against Freemantle. With impeccable arithmetic, just 100 years later, the club celebrated its centenary. They designated the league fixture against Everton on 30th November 1985 as the "Centenary Game."

Unfortunately, it started to go wrong when the pitch was declared too wet for 100 school children to form "100" on it and then a hot air balloon failed to get airborne. However, things picked up when the team ran out onto the pitch to a guard of honour formed by the school children. In the game, Glenn Cockerill scored in the first minute against the then current league champions. Things would not end on a high for Saints though. Everton equalised through Gary Lineker and although Steve Moran restored the lead in the 70th minute, Everton pushed on to win 2-3 with goals from Heath & Steven to poop the Saints party.

Centenary Game team:
Shilton; Baker(S.) Holmes, Case, Wright, Bond, Whitlock, Moran, Cockerill, Armstrong Wallace. Att.16,917. (Slightly above that seasons average of 15,034 but way below the capacity of approx 22,000.)

Championships

In the early days of professional football, the Football League catered for the Northern Clubs. The Southern League was the division for teams south of Birmingham. In Southampton's first Golden period between 1896 and 1904, they won the Southern League title six times in eight years.

After the First World War, a number of Southern League clubs were admitted to an enlarged Football League. Saints haven't fared quite so well in the Championship stakes since. The club won the Division

Three South title in 1921/22 on goal average, having finished equal on points with Plymouth Argyle. The only other Championship came in 1959/60 when they won the Third Division Championship with Norwich City runners-up.

Mick Channon (FA Cup Hero)

Undoubtedly one of the greatest players ever to have played for the Club. Legend has it that Ted Bates arrived at Channon's family house on Salisbury Plain and refused to leave until the 15-year-old had signed for Southampton.

Progress was swift and he became the youngest-ever player to appear in the reserves, before making his first team debut at 17 and scoring, as Saints beat Bristol City. As the club gained promotion, Mick was a regular in the side before his 19th birthday .

His first spell at the club saw Channon gain England caps and also captain his country, not to mention that 1976 FA Cup appearance. Although Channon had remained loyal to Saints after relegation in 1974, the prospect of a fourth year of Second Division football was too much. It was a mutual decision that he should move on to Manchester City in 1977, for a £300,000 fee.

Channon didn't enjoy a great spell at City and a little over two years

Mick Channon in action for Saints in 1974

Mick Channon and Dave Watson share a pot of tea in the dressing room at the Dell

later, he returned to the Dell. Channon's England career came to end during his time with Manchester City. In all he made 46 appearances, scoring 21 goals for the national side. Saints had been promoted back to the top division by the time Mick returned and some say he played his best football in this time, as he enjoyed a two-season partnership alongside Kevin Keegan.

Certainly Mick's best goal for the club was his last, a passing move that started at the back and involved nearly every member of the team before he volleyed home and displayed his famous windmill celebration for the last time in Saints colours.

Approaching 34, it was no surprise that Lawrie McMenemy let him go, and his free transfer was seen as more of a reward than as a reflection of his play. He spent a month at Newcastle United, playing four games, before another brief, nine game, spell with Bristol Rovers.

He had a significant swansong at Norwich City, though, winning a League Cup medal in 1985 before - and whisper it - joining his old mucker Alan Ball at Fratton Park. But his heart was always at the Dell and he retired in 1986. He played a starring role as a pundit in ITV's coverage of the Mexico World Cup, his Wiltshire burr and pronunciation of Gary "Loinaker" being the subject of much hilarity.

One story sums up Mick Channon's easy-going style. It's alleged that, in response to a Lawrie McMenemy rollicking one half time, Channon had looked up and said, "What you have got to understand gaffer, is this is only my f***** hobby."

Never was a truer word said in jest. Mick gave up his hobby and went to his first love of horse racing.

He became a licensed trainer in 1990 and now has some 200 horses at his stables near Newbury. In the sport of kings, Mick Channon is now one of the top trainers in the country.
602 (5) Apps. 228 goals.

Charity Shield

After winning the FA Cup in 1976, Saints met Liverpool in the Charity Shield in front of 76,500 at Wembley. They put out the same side that won the Cup in May. Saints were outplayed for most of the game and went down to a John Toshack goal.

The occasion was marred by disgraceful scenes after the presentation. Saints supporters, gathered at the tunnel end of the stadium, showing little charity, hurled missiles at the Liverpool players as they attempted to leave the pitch.

Martin Chivers

If you don't ask, you don't get. As a youngster, locally-born Chivers wrote to Southampton asking for a trial. He was taken on by the club and made his debut aged just 17 against Charlton Athletic in September 1962.

He quickly established himself and over the next five years his goals helped fire Saints into the top flight. He hit 30 in the promotion season, 1965/66. Incredibly all goals came in the first 29 games of the season and he failed to find the net in the run in.

A regular in the England U-23 side, there were many who raised eyebrows when Ted Bates sold him to Spurs in January 1968 for a then record British transfer fee of £125,000. The shrewd manager had his replacement already at the club, in Mick Channon.

Despite being only 22 when he left, Martin had made 189 starts plus one as a substitute. In that appearance from the bench, in April 1967, he became the first Saints substitute to score a goal. He had a long career at Spurs gaining 24 England caps, scoring 13 goals.
1962-68. 189 (1) Apps. 106 goals.

Chocolate Boxes

Mention Chocolate Boxes to any Saints fan over the age of 35 and they know you are referring to only one thing (well three actually) - the raised platforms of terracing that were erected at the back of the Milton Road terrace in the 1950s.

As Saints had nowhere to go in extending the ground, they built these quirky structures to expand capacity. There was nothing like them anywhere else in the country. Split into three sections, the right section was the biggest. For most of its life it had the name of a local sports shop "Toomers" emblazoned across it. Next to that in the middle, was the "boys pen" at the ground, and then tucked away in the East corner was the third and final part of the jigsaw.

The Chocolate Boxes were a rite of passage for most schoolboy fans. You started off first in the boys pen, progressing to the wall at the front of the terracing, and then on to other parts of the ground as you got older and presumably, taller.

From the 1960s onwards, beneath the Toomers box became Southampton's Kop, as the "Milton Mob" took residence, using what little cover there was, to try and emulate bigger covered ends.

It was a sad day for many when the Chocolate Boxes were demolished in 1981.

Club Crest

Early pictures of Southampton show varying badges on their shirts derived from the Hampshire county crest. However, when the club changed to the now familiar striped kit, the club formally adopted a shield taken from the Southampton Borough coat of arms. It featured three Tudor roses, and was used in the club programme, stationery and even club blazers, but it never appeared on the shirts.

Bill Ellerington in front of the Chocolate Boxes

In the 1974/75 season, the club decided to create a new modern crest and held a competition amongst supporters to design a new badge. The winning entry is still used till this day.

Its design can be briefly explained thus: at the base you have the name of the club; above, the City of Southampton is represented by the white rose on red background; above this we have the waves showing Southampton's connections to the sea and a tree denoting the other boundary, the New Forest; above that is a red and white scarf to represent the supporters, topped by a football to signify the game the club plays; with this being topped by a halo to remind everyone of the club's nickname.

Many fans think the design has remained constant to this day, but they aren't quite correct. The original design featured a plain white ball, but in 1997 Saints needed to copyright the design, so they made a subtle alteration, with the ball now featuring black spots.

CMFG

Any Saints supporter who attended games in 2002 will immediately remember exactly what the letters CMFG stand for: "Chris Marsden Football Genius."

In truth, Marsden's first couple of years at St Mary's after his arrival in 1999, were pretty unremarkable. Indeed, he only appeared in about half of the games in his first two seasons.

Then in 2001, came a career changing moment for the 33-year-old, folically challenged midfielder. Manager Gordon Strachan moved him to the left flank to partner Wayne Bridge, instead of moving him to another club. It was a master stroke.

Bridge had the pace and Marsden had the guile, and he seemed to grow in stature and revel in his new role. So much so, that at Ipswich in March 2002, he suddenly found skills that surprised the crowd and probably shocked himself.

He picked up the ball on the left, dropped his shoulder, glided past two defenders, rounded the goalkeeper and tapped the ball into the empty net. It nearly went wrong though, as he only just tapped it hard enough and it was almost cleared by a despairing Ipswich defender, but it trickled in and the fans had a new name for him.

The following season was probably Marsden's best ever, as the Saints stormed to the FA Cup Final. It was CMFG who lead the team out. Sadly, the "Bald Beckenbauer" wouldn't be the second man to lift the Cup for Saints and with the sale of Bridge in the summer of that year to Chelsea, Marsden's days at Saints were numbered.

After only 17 games in the following season Chris was allowed to seek his fortune abroad on a free transfer granted for services rendered. He played very briefly in South Korea before he returned to his home town of Sheffield to join Wednesday for a final few games, before retiring in 2005.
1999-04. 137 (15) Apps. 8 goals.

Colours

Saints have always played in red and white, although it hasn't always been in the striped design they are famous for. In their first four seasons from 1885, they played in white shirts with a red sash. Within three years they had actually got the sashes all going in the same direction.

Then from 1889, they adopted a design consisting of red & white quarters, and they would turn out in this until 1896 season, when the famous stripes were first worn. They

Southampton with their multi-directional sashes

celebrated the fact by taking up residence at the County Ground, winning the Southern League title for the first time and being unbeaten in the league.

With slight variations in the crazy kit era of the late 1970s/80s the design has been largely the same ever since. The width of the stripes being the most obvious variation. In 2003-04, the club produced a special European kit with narrow stripes. It was worn just twice, in the home and away games against Steaua Bucharest. Since 1999-00, Southampton have designed and produced their own kit.

Crossing The Divide

A total of 51 players have played for both Southampton & Portsmouth(correct up to September 2007).

Of that total, 31 of those have been by direct transfer between the two clubs whilst the remaining 20 have plied their trade elsewhere in between.

Saints have sent 18 players eastwards. Martin Cranie moving from St Mary's to Fratton Park in the summer of 2007 being the latest. Prior to Cranie, the last player to move East was Scott Hiley back in December 1999, whilst coming the other way in the past two seasons alone Saints have brought Nigel Quashie, Ricardo Fuller and John Viafara along the M27 in the best direction to travel and Portsmouth are catching up in the transfer stakes having sold Saints 15 players in total.

In truth, of the players that have transferred directly, it has generally been the Saints-bound players who have been successful, especially in the past three or four decades. Whilst the Saints crowd tends to be more tolerant that its Fratton counterparts and accepts that ex-Pompey players are only trying to better themselves and should be applauded for doing so, Pompey fans find it harder to accept ex-Saints into their fold.

The Skates would claim this is passion, although they showed no such passion in accepting the only Manager to make the direct move, firstly branding Harry

Redknapp a Judas for trading Fratton for St Mary's in December 2005. Some so-called supporters going as far as to issue death threats when Saints went to Fratton in April 06.

However they proved that in truth they are as willing as the next man to accept a so called Scummer when Harry left St Mary's in December 2006 to return to his "spiritual home" that is of course his spiritual home after West Ham, Bournemouth and a pie & mash shop in Barking.

Direct Transfers

Pompey To Saints
John Bainbridge
William Beaumont
Robert Blyth
Ricardo Fuller
Willie Haines
Barry Horne
Bert Houlker
John McIlwarne
Jerry Mackie
Nigel Quashie
Bill Rochford
Isaac Tomlinson
John Viáfara
John Warner

Riccardo Fuller

Saints To Pompey
Tommy Bowman
Arthur Chadwick
Eamonn Collins
Martin Crainie
Ron Davies
C. B. Fry
Paul Gilchrist
Alex Glen
Ivan Golac
Scott Hiley
Ted Hough
Alan McLoughlin
Steve Middleton

C.B. Fry

George Molyneux
Matthew Robinson
Bobby Stokes
John Warner

From Other Clubs
Ian Baird
Dave Beasant
John Beresford
Eyal Berkovic
Arthur Brown
Mick Channon
Colin Clarke
Andy Cook
Peter Crouch
Mervyn Gill
Jon Gittens
Trevor Hebberd
Bill Kennedy
George Lawrence
John Lewis
Alex McDonald
Harry Penk
Matt Reilly
Gregory Vignal
Malcolm Waldron
Ernest Williams

Trevor Hebberd

Harry Penk

Cup Finals
Saints have appeared in numerous and various Cup Finals over the years since winning the Hampshire Junior Cup back in 1887/88. However, we shall keep the list compact to those competitions of a senior level.

FA Cup
Saints played in their first FA Cup Final on April 21st 1900 when they lost 4-0 to Bury. A 75,000 crowd at the old Crystal Palace ground, saw the annihilation, as Southampton conceded three goals in the first 20 minutes and never recovered. Rumour had it that internal bickering between English and Scottish players in the side, had led to disharmony.

Their second final was only two years later when they met Sheffield United in front of 74,479 at the same

Saints' 1902 FA Cup Final team

venue. This time it was a lot closer. Saints fell behind but equalised through Harry Wood despite Yorkshire protests that he was offside.

The Replay nine days later was played on a bitterly cold day and this, as well as it being midweek, combined to reduce the crowd to only 40,000. Goalkeeper Robinson slipped to allow United the lead and although Brown equalised, another goalkeeping error sent the Cup to Sheffield with only six minutes left.

It would be another 74 Years before Saints played in another FA Cup Final. This time they made no mistake, beating Manchester United at Wembley on May 1st 1976, with a Bobby Stokes goal seven minutes from time.

The last FA Cup Final appearance to date came in 2003, when the game against Arsenal became the first to be effectively played "indoors." The roof at the Millennium stadium at Cardiff was closed for the first time at an FA Cup Final. Sadly, it was to no avail as the 73,726 crowd saw Arsenal win it. A goal from Pires was enough, despite a spirited late rally from Saints.

League Cup
Saints only appearance in the final came in 1979, when they met Nottingham Forest at Wembley in front of 100,000. Despite taking the lead through David Peach and leading at half time, Forest hit back with three goals.

A brace from Garry Birtles and one from Tony Woodcock being too much for Saints, despite a late goal from Nick Holmes.

Anglo Italian Cup
As Cup winners in 1976, Saints were invited to contest the Anglo Italian Cup Final with Napoli in a two-legged affair. The first leg at the Dell saw Steve Williams give Saints a 1-0 first leg lead in front of a 14,301 crowd.

The second leg was nearly two months later and was thought to be the first time Southampton had played a first team game on a Sunday. 60,000 turned out in Naples to see the tie all-square on aggregate by half time. However, Saints spirited resistance was broken in the final 20 minutes, and they conceded three goals to lose 4-0 on the night and 4-1 on aggregate.

Zenith Data Systems Cup
Saints reached the final in 1992, under Ian Branfoot, and a crowd of 67,688 turned out to see Saints face Nottingham Forest. The game was a repeat of the club's last visit to the twin towers.

Sadly, the result would be exactly the same. Saints came back from 2-0 down at the break to force extra-time with goals from Kevin Moore and Matt Le Tissier, but in the second period of extra time Scott Gemmill won the game for Forest. The match was the last ever final of the competition.

Texaco Cup
In the early 1970s, the Texaco Cup was a hotly contested challenge between English clubs and Scottish ones, on an invitational basis.

After winning their group and beating Glasgow Rangers in the semi-finals of the 1974/75 competition, Saints faced the not-very-Scottish Newcastle United in a two-legged final. 17,100 turned out for the first leg at The Dell to see Mick Channon give Saints a 1-0 first-leg lead.

However, despite controlling the second game for long spells, a late Newcastle goal took the game to extra time. The sending off of Jim Steele saw Saints lose their grasp of the game and concede a further two goals to lose the final.

Ron Davies in action for Saints in 1968

D
Ron Davies

Older Saints fans will tell you the greatest centre forward in the club's history was Ron Davies. Renowned as the greatest header of the ball of his era, it was said that he would literally hang in the air and wait for it to come. He did have the advantage of having one of the greatest crossers of the ball on the wing beside him though, in Terry Paine.

In his first season with Southampton, 1966-67, the first for the club in the top flight, he was the First Division's top scorer with 37 goals. He repeated the feat the following year, this time with a mere 28.

Perhaps his greatest day for the club though, was in August 1969, when Davies got all four in Saints 4-1 win at Old Trafford. It prompted Sir Matt Busby to proclaim him, "The finest centre forward in Europe," and to make repeated attempts to prise him away from the Dell.

Davies stayed until March 1973, when at 31, and despite a respectable 9 goals in 24 games he made his final bow for the club in his one appearance as a league substitute. It wasn't however to be his final game or goal at the Dell.

After joining Portsmouth he wore the number nine shirt in the first competitive South Coast Derby for eight years in September 1974. He scored a 59th minute penalty that unfortunately, for him at least, was upstaged by his successor Peter Osgood's late winner.

Ironically Ron finally did get a move to Old Trafford in November 1974. He was never to start a game, making eight appearances off the bench in the Red Devils' Second division championship-winning season.

Ron now lives in New Mexico working as a tiler despite needing a hip operation as he approaches retirement.
1966-73. 277 (4) Apps. 153 goals.

Eric Day

Eric had been spotted by Saints as early as 1941 whilst playing for the RAF. He was promptly offered a contract, but before he could sign, the War had other plans for him. He was involved in the D-Day invasions. As hostilities neared their end, he contacted the club to see if they were still interested.

After a couple of trial games, Eric finally made his league debut in November 1946 at the age of 25, some five years after he had come to Saints attention. Over the next dozen years he was to give Saints sterling

Eric Day

service, topping the Division Three goalscoring charts for three consecutive seasons.

Despite interest from several big London clubs he remained loyal to Saints. In his final season he went part-time before playing his last game in May 1957, as he approached his 36th birthday.

Eric Day is sixth in the list for the club's all-time goalscorers. He always followed the club's fortunes and was present for the final dinner at the Dell in 2001.
1946-57. 422 Apps. 156 goals.

The Dell

When first opened on 3rd September 1898, The Dell was considered one of the finest grounds in the country and it was to be the club's home for the next 103 years. By the end of its life it was the smallest ground in the Premier League, with the worst facilities. Saints fans loved it all the same.

Opening Match at The Dell, Southampton, 1898

The Dell was sited on land that Southampton director George Thomas purchased in 1898, only a few hundred yards from the County Ground. The only problem was that it included a lake that needed to be filled in, as well as two wooded banks and an ancient spring used in medieval times to serve the town.

The work was completed quickly and stands erected at a cost of £10,000 and Saints became the £250 per annum tenants, the mayor kicking off the first game against Brighton on September 3rd 1898, the result being 4-1 to the home side in a season that would end with Saints being crowned Southern League champions for the third year in a row.

Action from the first round of the FA Cup at the Dell, Southampton v. Everton, January 27th, 1900. Saints won 3-0

But if Saints thought their ground problems were over then they were wrong. In 1906 the lease was up for renewal and Mr Thomas proposed a 21 year lease but with the rent doubled to £500. The problem for Saints was that up to this point they had been the dominant club South of Birmingham. A string of Southern League titles allied with the two FA Cup Finals had seen a boom time. However the Southern League had imposed a wages cap and this had sent many of the better professionals in the South scurrying up North for better pay. The hike in rent couldn't have come at a worse time.

A compromise was reached and £400 per year agreed, but Saints struggled to meet the payments as their fortunes nose-dived. After the First World War, however, entry to the League heralded better days and when the current lease ended in 1926, the club bought the ground off the widow of George Thomas for £26,000.

On the other side of the ground, the East Stand was in need of renewal, but the Club could not afford the cost. Tongues wagged when, only hours after the final home game of 1928/29 season, it burned down. However, it could not be proven that the fire was anything other than an accident. Its successor was in place for the opening game of the following season and survived till the last kick at the ground.

The club immediately undertook improvements and renowned architect Archibald Leith designed a new West Stand, a structure that, despite some modification from the Luftwaffe in 1941, remained virtually unchanged until 2001.

In November 1940, the pitch was flooded by the medieval spring and the club had to find alternative venues for home matches. A "home" cup tie was played at Fratton Park against Brentford.

With the Dell still not ready for the start of 1941/42 season, Saints kicked off at Pirelli's sports ground in Dew Road, Eastleigh, although this was for one game only.

The Dell became one of the first grounds to stage a competitive football match under floodlights when on 1st

The Dell under flodlights in the 1960s

October 1951, a bumper crowd of 13, 654 saw a reserve team fixture with Spurs.

If the side stands were to remain constant, it was a different case behind the goals. Initially after being rebuilt following the war, and the addition of the "Chocolate Boxes" in the 1950's there was a period of stability at the ground. For three decades it remained pretty much the same.

Then in 1980, the Archers Road End was rebuilt. The terracing was dropped several feet so that supporters behind the goal could now actually see the goal line. The Milton Road End followed in 1981 and a two-tiered structure appeared in its place.

Neither were suitable for converting into seating, as the recommendations of the Taylor report came into force. First to go was once again, the Archers Road End in 1993. This was replaced by a smaller, covered structure, dubbed the Bike Shed by some wag. It was the turn of the Milton a year later and the stadium had taken on its final form.

Dell Timeline

1898. The Dell built at a cost of £10,000. Officially opened on September 1st with a League game against Brighton United, it consists of two single-tiered grandstands on each side, each holding 2,000 with open terracing on all four sides for 20,000.

1899. Estimated crowd of 23,000 watches Saints take on Derby County in FA Cup.

1921-23. General ground improvements including extending the East stand and installing seats and the rebuilding of the terracing behind the goal.

1927. Old West Stand, including the secretary's house which backed onto pitch demolished and new stand designed by Archibald Leith erected in place. Capacity was 4,500 in upper tier seating and 8,500 in terracing below. The official capacity of the ground is given as 33,000. This stand would remain virtually unchanged till 2001.

1929. Only hours after the final game of the season the East Stand mysteriously burns to the ground. A new stand is constructed in Liverpool and transported south. Basically a smaller version of the West stand.

Official league record crowd of 25,934 watches Spurs on Boxing Day. Ground Capacity is now estimated at 35,000.

Above: The Milton Road End is demolished in 1981. Right: The Archers End is fenced in 1978

1937. 30,380 watch Sunderland in the FA Cup third round to set new ground record.

The Milton Road end, circa 1989

1940. Luftwaffe, under direct orders from Hitler himself, bomb The Dell leaving a massive crater in the Milton penalty area, breaching the underground stream and flooding the pitch under 2ft of water.

1941. Unbeknown to most, the West Stand was used by the RAF to store "material" and in March it went up in flames. At the time, it was claimed to be an incendiary bomb during an air raid.

1949. The much-lamented "Chocolate Boxes" were constructed at the Milton Road end of the ground. Simply three raised platforms of terracing to the rear of the terrace. The ground, apart from the addition of floodlights, would be virtually unchanged for 31 years.

1950. Floodlights installed at a cost of £700. Initially

just used for training, then an experimental game against Bournemouth watched by 10,000.

1951. On the 1st October the first official match in England was played under the Dell lights when Spurs visited for a reserve team game.

1964. New gymnasium and club offices built behind West Stand.

1964. West & East Stand roofs reinforced to take new floodlight stanchions.

1969. Official record attendance against Manchester United - 31,044

Ted Bates closes the gates of The Dell for the final time in 2001

1978. Fence hastily erected at Archers Road end to pen in Spurs fans for the final game of season.

During the summer the fence is rebuilt and terrace is divided into four pens to better segregate rival fans. Bench seating is installed in the under east stand terrace area Milton wing and a television gantry built on the roof of the West Stand. Capacity now approximately 26,000 for return to top flight.

1979. Under West Stand, Archers Wing converted to bench seating.

1980. Archers Road end demolished and new structure erected. Terrace is lowered so that for the first time most spectators can see the goal line. Capacity now 24,000.

1981. The Milton Road end is demolished and a new two-tiered structure holding 7,500 erected in its place.

As with the opposite end the terracing is lowered, allowing fans unhindered views. Capacity back up to 25,000

1984. First live match on TV at The Dell against Liverpool March 16th. Two Danny Wallace goals secured a 2-0 win.

1986. Close-circuit TV installed in time for visit of Millwall.

1989. Hillsborough disaster brings in new regulations. Official capacity now barely 21,000.

1993. Bench seating and terracing under both East & West stands replaced by plastic seats. The Archers Road, built only 13 years before, demolished and replaced by an all seated structure holding only 1,400. Soon to be dubbed the Bike Shed. Capacity now approx 20,000.

1994. The Milton Road end is demolished, bringing an end to standing at Saints matches after 109 years. It's replaced by a 2,897 all-seater stand in a ground whose capacity is now only 15,200.

2001. May. The Dell sees its final games. Three in a week, to be precise, as firstly Arsenal are the visitors for the final League game, followed by Jason Dodd's testimonial. Finally, a friendly against Brighton, after which a capacity crowd literally tears the place down, helping themselves to anything that can be removed, aided by stewards and Police whose only job is to make sure no one gets hurt.

June/July. A supporters' six-a-side tournament is followed up by a black tie dinner on the pitch and an auction of memorabilia. Ted Bates fittingly locks the gates for the last time.

The ground is demolished and luxury housing built .

Dell Diamonds

As Saints prepared to leave The Dell and St Mary's started to rise from a building site near the Itchen river, The Daily Echo held a poll and invited its readers to vote for their favourite Saints players and managers of all time.

Understandably recent figures featured strongly and the voting was widespread, so much so that a clear winner was hard to choose. One thing it did reveal though, was the wealth of talent that had appeared in the red & white stripes over the years (well some of them had worn something that could loosely be described as stripes in the 1980s).

In commemoration of the poll the paper and the club produced a picture depicting the winners in full, who were as follows.

Jim Steele, Peter Osgood, Peter Rodrigues, Mark Dennis, John Sydenham, Jimmy Case, Charlie Wayman, David Armstrong, Peter Shilton, Matthew le Tissier, Bobby Stokes, Kevin Keegan, Ron Davies, Mick Channon, Chris Nicholl, Lawrie McMenemy,

Steve Williams, Ted Bates, Martin Chivers, Alan Ball, Alan Shearer, Mark Wright, Terry Paine, Nick Holmes.

So there you have it. Perhaps the 24 most influential men who have shaped the history of Southampton Football Club, post war at least.

Of course, there are some notable omissions, but all in all there probably isn't one Saints fan who would deny the right of any of those named to appear on that picture. After all, these were the men voted for by the very people who are the lifeblood of the club, the supporters.

Derbies

For Saints fans and those of Pompey too, come to that, there is only one derby and that's the one between Southampton and Portsmouth, first played in September 1899. The game was a friendly between the sides at Fratton Park, a 2-0 win for the home side.

Since then there have been a total of 212 fixtures played between the first teams including friendlies and minor competitions and the tally stands at 83 wins for Saints, 96 for Pompey and 33 draws.

However, as we all know it's only competitive games that count. Since the First World War the two clubs have been in the same division on surprisingly few occasions. Indeed between 1920/21 season, when both clubs joined the football league and 2007, a period spanning around 80-odd seasons (with a break for the war), the two were only in the same division on 15 occasions.

Saints fans will be pleased to know that out of 67 competitive games played, Southampton have won 34, Pompey 20 with 13 drawn, the goal tally is 109 for Saints and only 84 for Pompey.

Despite its relatively rare appearance on the fixture list over the years, the rivalry between the two sets of fans is as intense as anywhere else in the country. It has to be said that crowd violence has been a major worry at every fixture since the mid 1960s, meaning that most

Hampshire Policemen start to plan their holidays when the fixture list comes out.

Older Saints fans particular like to remember the FA Cup tie at Fratton Park in 1984. In the stoppage time allocated - due to Mark Dennis being hit by a coin thrown by a Pompey supporter - Steve Moran hit a last gasp winner to send 12,000 visiting fans wild.

Ali Dia

There can't be a football fan in the country that hasn't heard the name of Ali Dia. Surely the most infamous player ever. However, over the years, the story has become more myth that truth, so here we put the record straight.

In 1996-97 season, Saints manager Graeme Souness took a phone call. The caller offered him Dia, claiming that the Senegalese-born player was recommended by World Footballer of the Year, George Weah. Souness agreed to take him on trial, and this is where the story hots up.

Before Souness could even see Dia play in a training session, Saints suffered an injury crisis, meaning that Dia was signed on a temporary contract quickly. He was named as one of the substitutes in the home game against Leeds United in November 1996.

Matt Le Tissier suffered an injury in the 32nd minute and had to be replaced, and it was Dia who trotted on for his debut. It has to be said that Souness didn't have to use Dia. He also had Robbie Slater on the bench, so the manager can't be completely blameless in this farce.

In truth, the story could have been a lot different. With his first kick, Dia almost scored. Only a smart save from Nigel Martyn prevented a dream start. Souness must have had dreams of drawing up a three-year contract for the player. But no.

From there on in, it was clear that Dia hadn't a clue. He ran around aimlessly. Curiouser still, Oakley was replaced by Slater a good quarter of an hour before Dia

The (in)famous Ali Dia

himself was substituted in the 85th minute to end his 53 minutes of infamy.

Within 24 hours Dia was on his way. Next on his travels was a trial at Gateshead United. He failed even to make the grade there.

Folklore has it that Dia was only on the pitch a matter of minutes. It was a bit longer than that, and it has to be said it would take a brave man to mention the name of Ali Dia to Graeme Souness.

Diary Of A Season

Published in 1979, it was exactly as stated on the cover. The diary of Saints manager Lawrie McMenemy during the club's first season back in the top flight 1978/79. Fairly groundbreaking at the time, it gave a good insight into the everyday workings of a professional football club.

Fans, however, might be excused for sensing that it was a little bit watered down, from the fact that there wasn't one swear word in it!

The best section details a crucial team talk on the pitch before extra-time against West Bromwich Albion in a cup replay. Winger Terry Curran puts his hand up for permission to run off to the toilet! Today's player would want a limo brought on to take them.

The book obviously sold well in Southampton but would have limited appeal elsewhere. Looking at the book today, the hardback version cost £5.25 some four times the price of a terrace ticket at the Dell that season of 65p. It was an expensive read for a football fan

Jason Todd takes the applause at his testimonial

Jason Dodd

Jason Dodd wasn't strictly part of the youth team set up, having signed from Bath City as an 18-year-old in April 1989. But most would consider him as being developed by Saints. Within six months of his arrival, he had made his first team debut and for the next 15 years he was a first team regular, injuries permitting.

Sadly for such a great servant, two spells of injury coincided with perhaps the two biggest games in his time at the club. Firstly he missed out on a Wembley appearance in the Zenith Data Cup Final of 1992, and then the FA Cup Final of 2003 at the Millennium Stadium.

In the relegation season of 2004/05 Jason found himself ostracised by manager Harry Redknapp. Loan players, with no passion for the club, were getting selected over the likes of Dodd. He was released by Redknapp at the end of that season with barely a word of thank you. A

spell at Brighton followed, although age and injury was catching up with him and he retired from League football in the summer of 2006. He joined local Conference South side Eastleigh as firstly a player and then manager.

The good news for Saints supporters though was that in the summer of 2007 he returned to the club as first team coach.

1989-05. 454 (30) Apps. 13 goals.

Dogs

Perhaps one of the most bizarre incidents at the Dell happened during half time of the match against Norwich City in November 1978.

It was the annual visit to Southampton of the RAF police dog display team. Before the match, the dogs had gone through the usual display of climbing over obstacles and leaping through burning hoops. All very relevant if they have to chase an escaping arsonist through a children's playground. This was followed at half time with a demonstration of how a dog could chase and bring down an escaping villain.

The scene is this. A man with a briefcase walks across the pitch, only to be attacked by a man wearing a striped t-shirt, mask and an unfeasibly large right forearm. After the "thief" runs off with the case, the hound is released to chase him and bring him down, holding him till help arrives. Come to think of it, Saints could do with him in the team.

However, on this day, the villain must have had thespian ambitions, because not content with merely snatching the case and running, he decided to give his victim a bit of a beating for good measure. Acting of course, don't forget.

Enter one Police officer, who it can only be assumed, was lost in his perambulations of the perimeter track. He looked round to see two men fighting in the centre circle. Remember this was in the dark days of football hooliganism, so not beyond the realms of possibility.

The brave officer charged onto the pitch without a second thought for his own safety. He covered about 25 yards in record time

Perhaps it was the laughter of the crowd or maybe the Tannoy announcer shouting, "this is a RAF police dog display team demonstration. Will the police officer please leave the pitch" that caused him to realise what was happening.

He stopped and sheepishly left the crime scene, returning to the perimeter track. He continued his patrol to the cheers of the crowd, doffing his helmet in response as he left the arena to a lifetime of mickey-taking from his colleagues.

Ted Drake

Southampton born, Ted often recalled how he used to kick a ball around the streets of the town and dream of being the first Southampton born player to play centre forward for England. His dreams would be realised, but sadly he would have left The Dell to achieve them. He played a little over two years for Southampton before the lure of Arsenal and a record £6,000 transfer fee took him away from his home town in 1934.

In the 1930s he was a legend, leading both Arsenal and England up to the outbreak of the war. He scored seven goals in one game for the Gunners, a record that still stands. A talented sportsman, he did return home to play the odd game of cricket for Hampshire in the county championship.

After the war he entered management with Hendon, then Reading.

In 1952 he took over at Chelsea, leading them to their first League Championship in 1955. In the process, he became the first man to play in and then manage a title winning side. He was at Stamford Bridge nine years before joining the coaching staff at Fulham.
1931-34. 74 Apps. 48 goals.

E
Early Bath
Although it's quite common for players to hit the bath early after receiving a red card, it's not so common for managers. However in the 1984/85 season a fully clothed Lawrie McMenemy took a dip unexpectedly, when a dressing room argument with central defender Mark Wright got a bit out of hand.

As brawls of this nature are usually hushed-up, details are sketchy. But, by all accounts, Wright and McMenemy got pretty physical, with the big Geordie manager ending up, suit and all, in one of the baths in the changing room.

England International Games Staged
Southampton's home ground has been used to stage a full England international match on two occasions. The first, back on 1st March 1901, saw both goalkeeper Jack Robinson and C.B. Fry selected from the home side, as England defeated Ireland 1-0.

The second match on 16th October 2002, paired England with Macedonia in a European Championship qualifying game. Local lad made good, Wayne Bridge, featured in the game that ended 2-2, in front of a capacity crowd.

England U-21 Games Staged (The Dell):
v. Norway. 09/09/1980. Won 3-0
v. Finland. 16/10/1984. Won 2-0
v. Hungary. 11/09/1990. Won 3-1
v. Poland. 26/03/99. Won 5-0

England U-20 Games Staged (St Mary's):
v. Portugal. 22/11/2001. Won 1-0

England Internationals

A total of 27 players have represented England whilst playing for Southampton. The first was goalkeeper Jack Robinson who had already been capped when he joined Saints from New Brighton Tower in 1898. He became the club's first England international the following year, playing against Wales and Scotland - the first of six caps he gained whilst at the Dell.

Terry Paine was in the 1966 World Cup winning squad for England, winning the last of his 19 caps in the tournament against Mexico. He found himself surplus to requirements as Sir Alf Ramsey adopted his "wingless wonders" tactic.

Peter Shilton won the most England caps whilst at the Dell, appearing on no less than 49 occasions between 1982-87.

Perhaps the Saints man most would associate with the Three Lions, is Mick Channon, who gained 45 caps and scored 21 goals for the national side.

Possibly the best England connection was on 7th March 1981, when a Saints side playing against Manchester United at the Dell, contained no less than four England captains: Alan Ball, Mick Channon, Dave Watson and Kevin Keegan.
Keegan scored the winner in a 1-0 win. Just over a year later, two more England captains joined the club, in Peter Shilton & Mick Mills. Sadly, by then, the other

four had already left so six England captains in one team was not achieved.

England Internationals

J.W. Robinson	1899-1901	6 caps	
A. Turner	1900-1901	2 caps	
A. Chadwick	1900	2 caps	
C.B. Fry	1901	1 cap	
G. Molyneux	1902-1903	4 caps	
A.E. Lee	1904	1 cap	
A.E. Houlker	1906	2 caps	
W. Rawlings	1922-1923	2 caps	
F. Titmuss	1922-1923	2 caps	
T.R. Parker	1925	1 cap	
A. Ramsey	1948	1 cap	
W. Ellerington	1949	2 caps	
T. Paine	1963-1966	19 caps	7 goals
M. Channon	1972-1977	45 caps	21 goals
D. Watson	1979-1981	18 caps	1 goal
K. Keegan	1981-1982	9 caps	2 goals
P. Shilton	1982-1987	49 caps	
D. Armstrong	1982-1984	2 caps	
S. Williams	1983-1984	6 caps	
M. Wright	1984-1987	16 caps	
D. Wallace	1986	1 cap	1 goal
A. Shearer	1992	3 caps	1 goal
T. Flowers	1993	1 cap	
M. Le Tissier	1994-1997	8 caps	
W. Bridge	2002-2003	12 caps	
J. Beattie	2003	5 caps	
P. Crouch	2005	1 cap	

England B Internationals

Alf Ramsey	1948	1app.	
William Ellerington	1949	1app.	
Steve Williams	1979-81	4apps.	
David Peach	1979	1app.	
Malcolm Waldron	1979	1app.	
Matthew Le Tissier	1990-98	6apps.	3 goals.
Rod Wallace	1990	1app.	
Alan Shearer	1992	1app.	

England U-23 Internationals

John Sydenham	1959-60	2 caps
Terry Paine	1960-62	4 caps
Martin Chivers	1964-67	12 caps
Mick Channon	1970-72	9 caps
Steve Mills	1974	1 cap

England U-21 Internationals

David Peach	1977-78	8 caps
Steve Williams	1977-80	14 caps
Graham Baker	1980	2 caps
Steve Moran	1981-84	3 caps
Danny Wallace	1983-86	14 caps
Mark Wright	1983	4 caps
Tim Flowers	1987	3 caps
Neil Ruddock	1989	4 caps
Ray Wallace	1989	4 caps
Rod Wallace	1989-91	11 caps
Jason Dodd	1990-91	8 caps
Alan Shearer	1990-91	11 caps
Richard Hall	1992-93	11 caps
Neil Shipperley	1995	6 caps
Graham Potter	1996	1 cap
Matthew Oakley	1997-98	4 caps
Kevin Davies	1997-00	2 caps
James Beattie	1998-99	5 caps
Wayne Bridge	1999-01	7caps
David Prutton	2003-07	8caps
Andrew Surman	2004-	2caps

European Cup Winners Cup

Saints had one season in this now defunct competition, that was competed for by the winners of each domestic cup final winners.
Southampton took part in the 1976/77 season's cup.

In the first round, they met Olympic Marseille who were despatched 4-0 at the Dell before a 1-2 defeat in France sent Saints through 5-2 on aggregate.

The second round saw Saints drawn against Carrick Rangers from Northern Ireland. The away leg was first and the part timers were beaten 5-2 by a star studded Saints side.

The highlight of the game though, was when a Carrick player was carried off by stretcher, or rather, was attempted to be carried off. The stretcher bearers walked off in different directions, dumping the unfortunate player back on the turf. In the second leg, Saints completed the task with a 4-1 home win.

The quarter finals saw Saints paired with Belgian giants and holders Anderlecht. The first leg in Brussels saw Saints go behind in the 30th minute followed by a 82nd minute Rensenbrink second. Meanwhile, Mick Channon had what looked like a good goal ruled offside.

Many years later in 2001, when Anderlecht were convicted of bribing match officials in Europe. Saints manager in 1977, Lawrie McMenemy, reflected upon the dubious decision by the officials and rumours of bribery that had been rife after the game.

In the second leg, Saints had no choice but to go for the jugular and after David Peach pulled one back from the spot, Ted MacDougall brought the tie level on 79 minutes. With Saints on the attack, it looked like there would be only one winner. Then Jim Steele let a ball under his foot to let Van Der Elst score a late goal and Saints hopes were dashed.

European Tour

"We're all going on a European tour," the Saints players of 1900/01 might have been singing, although a look at the itinerary must have brought tears to the eyes. If it wasn't around the world in 80 days, it was definitely around Europe in ten.

Saints kicked off in Holland beating The Hague 6-2 on April 21st. Two days later and they were in Prague beating Slavia 5-1, followed by a win the next day over a combined Prague and Vienna XI 3-0.

It was then off to Vienna itself to beat Vienna C & FC 7-0 on the 27th, Vienna Combined 8-0 on the 28th, before a quick train journey to Budapest to meet Toma Club 8-0 on the 29th.

A day later and the final game was against a combined Hungarian XI, who despite meeting a side that must have been dead on its feet, still managed to see them off 13-0. And today's players think they have it tough with having to play two games a week occasionally.

Ever Presents

An impressive 49 players have gone through an entire league season ever present for Saints. The greatest number of seasons is seven, by Terry Paine, closely followed by Mick Channon with four.

In recent times, Wayne Bridge played in every league game in season 2000/01 and 2001/02, and was accompanied by Claus Lundekvam in the first of those seasons.

F

Family Centre

Southampton Football Club has always been known as a friendly place, but it's a little known fact that in 1977 Saints opened the first dedicated section of a ground for families only.

In 1977 the East side of the Milton End terrace was fenced off and reserved for those who purchased family tickets. So popular was it, that a year later the section was extended. With the rebuilding of the terrace in 1981, the Family Section moved to the upper tier of the new structure, enjoying probably the most spectacular view of the entire ground. Although being high up and open to the elements wasn't always an advantage.

After over a decade "up in the gods," so to speak, the Milton End was once more demolished for an all-seater stand in 1994. The Family centre was relocated once again, this time to the Milton Wing of the Under West Stand, a seated section. There it remained right up until the Dell was vacated in 2001.

In St Mary's, the Family Section is as busy as ever and

Saints fans in full regalia in 1993

located in the corner of the Kingsland and Chapel stands. Many clubs have laid claim to their family image, but surely none have as great a claim as Saints, who led the way in encouraging families to come to football in a completely safe atmosphere in a dedicated section of the stadium.

Fancy Dress

In the past decade or so, the wearing of fancy dress to the final away game of the season has become more of an occurrence, not just amongst Saints supporters but across the land. However, there can't be another club that took it to the extreme that Saints followers did and introduced an annual theme to proceedings.

The first real theme came in May 1993 for the visit to Oldham Athletic. The Lancastrians were surprised to see several hundred visiting fans dressed as Arabs in honour of Francis Benali. Benali himself must have been bemused, probably the nearest he had been to the Pyramids was a visit to the Swimming centre of the same name in Southsea.

With his dark complexion and bushy moustache, he was honoured as grown men wore tea towels and false moustaches. It was rumoured that someone had got hold of a camel and was bringing it to the game but sadly this was a hoax.

The following year saw a trip to West Ham in the final game and with so much at stake fancy dress went out the window, as it did for a couple of more years until Saints visited Aston Villa on the final day in 1997. West Country boy Micky Evans had come in and made his mark with some crucial goals in the run in. So he was duly honoured as fans gave their impressions of a country bumpkin in his honour, complete with straw and strips of carpet to imitate his bushy sideburns.

In 1999 came the greatest fancy dress day of them all as Saints took over Selhurst Park. It was Hassan Kachloul day and literally thousands donned fezzes and played kazoos as Saints ground-out a famous victory. To the home fans and neutrals it must have been surreal.

In 2002 it was Gordon Strachan who was honoured as the away programme once again ended at Villa Park. Tam o'Shanters with ginger wigs were abundant, with the occasional kilt making an appearance.

In 2003 the trip to Manchester City was low key, mainly due to it being the final game at Maine Road and only a thousand tickets being allocated to the club. But Chris Marsden was honoured with a variety of "bald" wigs.

In 2004 the trip to Charlton Athletic honoured keeper Antti Niemi, who ironically was injured for the game. He sportingly came to the away end, signed autographs and gave his shirt to a youngster. The Finn must have been bewildered to see an astonishing array of blond wigs in his honour.

Since then Saints fans haven't had a lot to laugh at come the end of the season, but hopefully a new hero will emerge soon and will find out that in these parts they have a strange way of showing that they like you.

Fanzines

The first-ever Saints fanzine hit the streets in 1987, as the fanzine movement picked up momentum and was entitled *Junk Mail*. This was soon followed by the strangely titled *Ugly Inside* in April 1988.

Junk Mail was short lived. However, "The Ugly" (as it became known) became the longest running Saints fanzine, still continuing to this day (see Ugly Inside). In early 1990 came a couple of new contenders. *Devalued*, bizarrely, originated from Oldham, written by a then 15-year-old schoolboy Ian Ellis. It was short on presentation and big on opinion, the true spirit of fanzines.

On the March had a lot more staying power than many fanzines at the time, although it seemed to take its cover design straight from *The Ugly*. Sadly its demise, when it came, was short and swift. After producing a cover featuring Saints boss Ian Branfoot with the caption "Hope you die soon," the editors realised that they had overstepped the mark and ceased publication in late 1993.

By then, however, a new name was on the block, *Red Stripe*, featuring an A5 format rather than the A4 favoured by most. *Red Stripe* was a good addition to the Saints fanzine stable. However, they too blotted their copybook slightly, by featuring the infamous "suicide pill" issue. Closer inspection, however, revealed nothing more than a Smartie taped to the cover.

Finally came *The Beautiful South* in the late 1990s. In a similar format to the rest, it found itself the last paper based fanzine as *The Ugly Inside* switched to internet only in 2000. However, it appeared sporadically over the next few years. The last edition came out in 2004 and since then St Mary's has lacked the sight of fanzine sellers selling their wares on the streets.

Perhaps the most significant contribution the Fanzines made to the Saints cause came in October 1993 when a meeting was held consisting of various fanzine editors at the Captains Corner public house. The main topic on the agenda was the universal dissatisfaction with then-manager Ian Branfoot.

A public meeting was called at the same venue a week later and a packed house saw the formation of the Southampton Independent Supporters Association and the campaign to oust Branfoot was born, succeeding three months later.

Father & Son

Sam Meston joined Saints in 1895 and over the next 11 years, turned out for the club in a variety of positions clocking up 246 games including the two FA Cup finals and scoring 18 goals in the process.

Meston arrived as part of the so called "Stoke invasion," as professional players from the North flocked South for better wages. His hard shot earned him the nickname "Long Tom."

His total of appearances was incredible in an age when footballers had even less loyalty to the club and more to the wallet than today's specimens. After retiring, he stayed in the area working as a brake fitter in the Eastleigh Railway works.

His son was also called Sam, although he was better known as Sammy. After making his debut in 1922 he at first looked to be following in the footsteps of his father. Sadly as he started to establish himself, he broke his leg.

He returned after a year, but during his comeback he had the misfortune to break the same leg and he was never the same player again.

He moved on to Gillingham after only 10 appearances and 2 goals. Surprisingly he got a move to Everton and even appeared alongside the great Dixie Dean in the season when the great man scored a record 60 league goals .

By the age of 29 he was back in Southampton and found employment as a bookies runner. Sam Senior died in Ashurst in 1948, aged 76. His son, however, only

just outlasted him dying prematurely of a heart attack in Woolston aged only 51.

Charlie McGibbon only had one season at the Dell in 1909/10, but he hit 19 goals in 28 games before moving on to Arsenal. His posting with the Royal Artillery, where he was a Sergeant, took him away before he could complete the season.

His son Doug made his League debut in 1939. Unfortunately it was the last game before the start of the Second World War. It robbed him of the best part of his career.

However, when the league restarted in 1946, Doug was in the side scoring a hat-trick as Saints beat Swansea Town 4-0. After waiting all that time to play his second game and with 11 goals in 15 games to his name, he was inexplicably sold to Fulham.

Charlie Sillett was a versatile player who captained Saints, making 183 appearances scoring 10 times between 1931-38. He left the club to play for Guildford and become mine host at the Lamb in Nomansland, famous as the pub where the Hampshire/Wiltshire boundary runs through the bar. In Charlie's time closing time was later in Wiltshire meaning that customers had to move to the other half of the pub late in the evening if they wanted to carry on drinking.

Sadly, Charlie was killed in the Second World War when the ship he was on, SS Corvus, was sunk off of the Isle Of Wight in March 1945.

His son Peter Sillett played 65 times for Saints scoring 4 times from the full back position. With Saints struggling financially after relegation, he was sold to Chelsea where he had a distinguished career including England caps.

Peter's younger brother John was on Saints books as well. Though he had not played first team football, he went to Stamford Bridge as part of the deal. John of course famously managed Coventry City to their FA Cup win in 1987.

Hugh Fisher (FA Cup Hero)

The unsung hero of the 1976 FA Cup winning side. There are many who will tell you that without Hugh, Saints would have never got their hands on the trophy. Signed from Blackpool in March 1967, Fisher went on to make 356 appearances for the club scoring 11 goals, but it would be his last goal that would be the most important.

Hugh Fisher

In the third round of that cup-winning season, Saints found themselves a goal down to Aston Villa at the Dell. With only seconds remaining on the clock, Fisher, who hadn't scored in 18 months, let fly from outside the box for a vital equaliser and the rest as they say, was history.

Unfortunately for Hugh, he would not feature at Wembley, finding himself on the bench for the full 90 minutes. He played in all the games up until the semi final with Crystal Palace. However, on the eve of this game, Hugh knew that he was feeling a little bit of a strain.

Whereas many on the cusp of such a big occasion would have kept quiet and played, Hugh, ever the professional, told the manager of his injury. Paul Gilchrist stepped in to replace him and scored the winner. Pictures of the game show Fisher celebrated from the bench.

For the final, it was the same combination. Saints fans owe a big debt to Hugh, who not only scored the goal that changed history, but put club interests before his own. After leaving Saints in March 1977, Hugh became

Southport player-manager. Sadly after his only full season at Haig Avenue, in the days of having to apply for re election to the league rather than automatic relegation, the Sandgrounders were voted out in favour of Wigan Athletic.

Hugh still lives in the Southampton area to this day, working in the Brewery trade.
1967-77. 356 (10) Apps. 11 goals.

Football League Review

In the late 1960s through to the mid 1970s, the Saints match day programme in common with many other clubs, featured an insert called The Football league Review.

While the club programme remained strictly black & white, apart from a smattering of red on the cover, the Review was a blaze of colour. The cynical would say that it enabled many clubs to get away with printing basic sub-standard programmes, knowing that the inclusion of the FLR made it good value for money.

In truth, it was worth the price of the programme for the FLR alone. Despite being an official League publication, it was almost a pre-prototype fanzine in content and was clearly aimed at the teenage supporter.

Regular features included a vote for "The most attractive hunk in football," and a letter page that was so surreal that surely only members of the Beatles entourage who met the Maharishi would understand it.

Saints famously featured in the "Make friends with other fans" feature when a female QPR fan wanted to meet up again with a Saints fan who she had quaintly let use her scarf to mop up the blood from his headwound. Presumably after a traditional 1969 spot of skinhead aggro on the terraces.

Freedom Of The City

After the FA Cup Final win in 1976, the club attended a Civic reception in their honour. Mayor Irene Candy awarded the club the Freedom Of The City Of

George Reader accepts the Freedom of the City on behalf of the club in 1976

Southampton, the greatest honour the City can bestow.

It does, however, offer only limited privileges nowadays. Apart from a parchment scroll to hang on your wall, it also includes the right to herd your sheep through the Bargate Arch, and as Saints fans would surely agree, its been a long time since anyone has done that.

Ted Bates also had the honour conferred on him individually in 2001, as did Matthew Le Tissier. Both gratefully accepted the honour, although to date, Le Tiss hasn't been seen buying up local supplies of sheep.

C.B. Fry

C.B. Fry was considered one of the great sportsmen of the modern era when he joined Southampton Football Club in 1900. Charles Burgess, as he was christened was born in 1872.

Athletically as well as academically gifted, he not only equalled the World long jump record in 1893 but was also considered one of the greatest cricketers in England in the late Victorian era, perfecting his talents at Oxford University (where else).

A talented right-handed batsman, Fry went on to captain both Sussex and England. As captain he never lost a Test Match. He scored over 30,000 first-class runs at an average of over 50. He was an outstanding sportsman, politician, teacher, writer, editor and publisher.

It was no surprise that he had little time to play football turning out for the Corinthians before joining Saints in 1900, still as an amateur. He insisted that he wore the striped socks of Corinthians in all games.

C.B. Fry

A gifted full back, his other pursuits meant that in his three seasons at Southampton, he only made 16 league appearances plus a total of 9 in the FA Cup. He did, though play in both the final and replay against Sheffield United in 1902. The same year, he made his only footballing appearance for England, against Ireland at the Dell.

After finishing his football career, Fry continued playing cricket for Sussex, Hampshire and England before retiring from competitive sport in 1921.

His achievements in so many fields won him many admirers, not least the people of Albania who offered him the throne of their country. In 1934, he met Adolf Hitler and, impressed by his charisma, was still expressing the German's virtues as late as 1938.

Fry tried and failed to persuade von Ribbentrop that Nazi Germany should take up the game of cricket to Test level. In later life he ran a training ship on the River Hamble for sea cadets. He died in 1956, aged 84.

Fund Raising

In the 1950s, as the team declined and attendances dropped, Southampton was lucky in that it had a strong Supporters Club. It was founded in 1926 with a motto of "To help not to hinder." Based at The Bedford Hotel, known to all now as just The Bedford, the club held monthly dances and match day draws to win a ball or season ticket. Certainly the football club itself was grateful for its existence. In 1949, it approached the Supporters Club to help finance the erection of floodlights.

Further help came in 1956 when the club had debts of £23,032 and no money for players. The supporters club came to the rescue and financed the purchase of Jimmy Shields from Sunderland for the princely sum of £1,000.

The supporters club continued its fund raising, donating money mostly for ground improvements including a £2,000 donation to upgrade floodlights in 1960. Older fans will remember the "penny on the ball" tickets when you could win the match ball. They continued to the early 1970s, when, as football became big money, the club finally decided to take its fund raising in-house, with full time employees.

The first fruits of their labour were the Golden Goal competition. Quite simply, fans bought a ticket which they unveiled to reveal a time. If the first goal was scored at this time, then they won the jackpot or at least shared in it.

In 1976, after the FA Cup win, Saints introduced their "Treble Chance" draw, a weekly draw. An army of collectors went round to the subscribers each week and for their 10p they could win the grand prize of £50, two

smaller prizes and several consolation amounts. A year later and that was augmented by the 20p "Pools tickets," a forerunner of today's scratch cards. The official yearbook of 1978/79 shows that for 20p punters had the chance to win a £1,000 first prize, with another £3,000 up for grabs in smaller amounts.

In 1985 the club decided to end the Treble Chance and replace it with the Centenary Club Draw, an altogether more sophisticated affair. Members subscribed through a direct debit payment with the chance to win major prizes.

Coincidentally the first prize of £5,000 was won in March 1987 by Saints director and future Chairman Guy Askham and in the same draw the £500 prize was won by Lawrie McMenemy. It was all just coincidence apparently and no, they didn't put the money back in the pot.

Saints continued to raise funds in this manner until 1994 when the National Lottery was launched. The club found that this new draw cornered the market place. In 1990s football, the income from fund raising was just a drop in the ocean and they ceased their own activities.

G

Paul Gilchrist (FA Cup Hero)

Gilchrist was signed by Ted Bates in 1972 from Doncaster Rovers. Paul would be one of the least known and remembered of the 12 on duty at Wembley in 1976, but that shouldn't reflect his contribution to the cup run, in which he appeared in all but one of the games, scoring twice in the process.

His Champagne moment for Saints came in the semi final against Crystal Palace at Stamford Bridge. Ironically, he would probably have been on the bench if Hugh Fisher hadn't been injured. With the score deadlocked on 74 minutes, he let fly from 25 yards to open the scoring. Mick Channon has always claimed that it brushed his sock on the way in and that the goal should be his, but whatever the truth, it sent Saints on their way to Wembley.

Paul Gilchrist celebrates victory in the 1976 FA Cup semi-final

Gilly played in the final but he would play only four more games for the club afterwards, including the Charity Shield, as manager McMenemy started a complete overhaul of the team.

After four years at the Dell, he left for Portsmouth, Swindon and finally Hereford, where an injury ended his career in 1980, still aged only 29. He now lives in Kent where he is employed by BMW.
1972-76. 120 (13) Apps. 22 goals.

Goalkeepers

Saints have been lucky to have been blessed with a number of top class goalkeepers over the years. So many indeed, that a vote on the greatest ever keeper to have played for the club would be the catalyst for a mass argument in any bar where Saints fans were gathered.

In the early days it was Jack Robinson who made the headlines playing in our first two cup finals and being capped by England. In later years it would be Eric Martin – surely the greatest Scottish keeper never to win a cap for his country – who would be the fans' hero in the first spell in the top flight. Then again, Saints supporters were spoilt as Peter Shilton joined,

followed by Tim Flowers and Antti Niemi. All of them could lay claim to being Saints greatest ever keeper. Opinion will always be divided on the subject but it is fair to say that these three would always be high on anyone's list.

Peter Shilton
When he arrived at the Dell he was regarded as the best keeper in the world and was certainly the most capped Saints player for England, winning 49 caps during his stay. Methodical and serious, Shilton was admired and respected, rather than adored by Saints fans. During a five year stay with the club, he made 242 appearances before leaving for Derby County. He was still considered the world's number one keeper at the age of 38.

Tim Flowers
Flowers had been signed in the summer of 1986 after impressive displays for Wolves whilst still in his teens. He had an inauspicious start for Southampton,

Peter Shilton

Tim Flowers

conceding five on his debut at Old Trafford, followed a month or so later by being stretchered off after conceding a penalty with a fractured cheekbone. Nevertheless, he had an impressive spell deputising for Shilton at the end of his first season. After a dodgy start the next term, he found himself playing second fiddle to John Burridge for a couple of years. In 1989 he made the goalkeeper's spot his own and unlike Shilton, he was adored by the Dell faithful.

But after winning his first England cap in July 1993 Flowers' stock with Saints fans dropped. He left for Blackburn Rovers for £2million, then a world record fee for a goalkeeper.

Ironically he made his home debut for Blackburn against Southampton, milking the applause of his new paymasters and completely ignoring the travelling Saints fans. He was never received with warmth on his returns to the Dell – a shame, because with 252 appearances for the club in over 7 years, he was a great servant.

Antti Niemi

Niemi was allegedly signed grudgingly by Gordon Strachan, who was somewhat persuaded by chairman Rupert Lowe that Niemi was his man. It was soon clear that he was a great performer and it would be true to say he was the most popular keeper amongst the supporters that the club ever had.

With his trademark bleached blonde hair, he performed wonders for the team. His one flaw was that he was injury prone and in three and a half seasons he only managed 123 appearances – about two thirds of the games he could have played. He famously had to come off injured in the 2003 FA Cup Final. After relegation, Niemi remained loyal to the club and because of this the supporters waved him off to Fulham with their best wishes.

Goalkeepers capped by their country whilst with Saints

Jack Robinson	England
Peter Shilton	England
Tim Flowers	England
Ian Black	Scotland
Hugh Kelly	Northern Ireland
Fred Kiernan	Republic Of Ireland
Paul Jones	Wales
Antti Niemi	Finland
Bruce Grobbelaar	Zimbabwe

Southampton Goalkeepers, 1946-End Of 2006/07 Season

George Ephgrave	1946-48	38 apps
Len Stansbridge	1938-51	52 apps (incl pre war)
Ian Black	1947-50	104 apps
Hugh Kelly	1950-51	30 apps
Edwin Thomas	1950-52	8 apps
John Christie	1950-59	217 apps
Fred Kiernan	1951-56	136 apps
Mervyn Gill	1955-56	1 app
Brian Stevens	1956-59	13 apps
Tony Godfrey	1958-66	149 apps
Bob Charles	1959-61	35 apps
Ron Reynolds	1959-64	111 apps
John Hollowbread	1964-66	40 apps
Campbell Forsyth	1965-68	51 apps
David MacLaren	1966-68	26 apps
Gerry Gurr	1966-70	49 apps
Eric Martin	1966-75	289 apps
Sandie Davie	1970-72	1 app
Steve Middleton	1973-77	29 apps (+1 sub)
Ian Turner	1973-78	107 apps
Colin Boulton	1976 (loan)	6 apps
Jim Montgomery	1976 (loan)	5 apps
Peter Wells	1976-84	160 apps
Terry Gennoe	1978-80	51 apps
Ivan Katalinic	1979-82	54 apps

Peter Shilton	1982-87	242 apps
Phil Kite	1984-86	5 apps
Keith Granger	1985-88	2 apps
Tim Flowers	1986-93	251 apps
Eric Nixon	1986-87(loan)	4 apps
John Burridge	1987-89	75 apps
Ian Andrews	1989-94	10 apps
Dave Beasant	1993-97	107 apps
Bruce Grobbelaar	1994-96	45 apps
Neil Moss	1995-2002	24 apps (+2 sub)
Maik Taylor	1996-97	18 apps
Paul Jones	1997-2004	220 apps (+3 sub)
Antti Niemi	2002-2006	123 apps
Alan Blayney	2002-2006	3 apps
Kasey Keller (loan)	2004	4 apps
Paul Smith	2004-06	20 apps (+2 sub)
Bart Bialkowski	2006-Present	16 apps
Kevin Miller	2006-07	7 apps
Kelvin Davis	2006-Present	44 apps

Goalscorers

Top League Goalscorers
185	Mick Channon 1966-77 & 1979-82
161	Matthew Le Tissier 1986-2002
160	Terry Paine 1956-74
156	Bill Rawlings 1920-27
154	George O'Brien 1959-66
145	Derek Reeves 1955-62
145	Eric Day 1945-1957
134	Ron Davies 1966-73
97	Martin Chivers 1962-68
90	Tommy Mulgrew 1954-62

Top Goalscorer in one season
44   Derek Reeves 1959-60
(See also Individual Scoring Records)

The Great Escape

Season 1998/99 is remembered with much fondness by Saints supporters although for much of it, it wasn't very enjoyable at all. Indeed it would be the 10th game before Saints would chalk up a win, and the start of May before they would move any higher than 19th. but it would become known as the Great Escape.

By Christmas the task to stay up looked impossible. Saints had moved above Nottingham Forest in the table, but they were still along way off safety. The crunch game was the first of the New Year when fellow strugglers Charlton Athletic were the visitors. They were dispatched 3-1. It was a start, but still a long way to go.

The season then started to take on a pattern. Saints would win at home but lose away. Slowly but surely they started to gain ground on those around them. The visit of Blackburn was crucial, a real relegation six pointer. After an hour of the battle, though, Saints looked finished, 1-3 down. Blackburn's superstar players were taunting the crowd, then something happened.

Marian Pahars

The crowd wouldn't give up and neither would they let the players. Mark Hughes prodded in his only goal of the season and the tide turned. With nine minutes remaining substitute Marian Pahars headed his first goal for the club and it was all square. Blackburn weren't laughing now. Despite late pressure Southampton held on for a draw, but the Saints fans knew the season was changing. They sensed the players had the spirit and the Great Escape theme was sang with gusto.

A draw at Derby was the first away point picked up since December followed by a home win against Leicester that saw Saints pull above the bottom three for the first time all season with two games left.

Next up was an away game at Wimbledon. All ten thousand seats for the away terrace were snapped up immediately. Saints supporters were also buying tickets from the home club and Selhurst Park became Dellhurst Park with an estimated fifteen thousand visitors in a twenty four thousand crowd, with many more outside. It was a tense affair till the 72nd minute when Le Tissier came from the bench and changed the game.

Firstly a pin-point free kick found Beattie and then a Le God corner seemed to go directly in. (Robbie Earle would later be 'credited' with an own goal). In between, Saints cleared off the line when Francis Benali put the only thing he had to hand in the way of the ball, namely his testicles, and the Dons couldn't force the ball home.

The celebrations were tempered with the news that Charlton had scored a last minute winner at Villa. It would go to the last day.

Everton were the visitors to The Dell on the last day and it was a straight fight between Saints and Charlton for the last relegation place. Saints had 38 points and Charlton 36. There were several permutations, but in simple terms Saints could get away with a draw if Charlton won by less than four.

Pahars popped up to calm collective nerves on 24 minutes and when he added a second with 20 minutes to go, the crowd knew that only a drastic turnaround would see the team relegated. With ten minutes left, news came through that Charlton had gone a goal down to Sheffield Wednesday it was all over bar the singing. And sing Saints supporters did, as the Great Escape echoed around the ground.

The final table shows Saints five points above Charlton and close to mid-table obscurity, The table doesn't lie, but it also doesn't always tell the full story.

Grounds, Pre-St Mary's

Southampton St Mary's first ever club game was on November 21st.1885 on the site of what is now the Hampshire Bowling Club in Northlands Road.

Their first permanent home would be a few hundred yards away on the Avenue side of the Cowherds pond, and it was here on the Common that the majority of the club's first home games took place.

However it was not the ideal spot and matches were

Hampshire Bowling Club

sometimes held up to allow pedestrians to cross the pitch and this led club officials to look for a more permanent residence. They did not have to look far, as Hampshire Cricket Club had recently vacated what was known as the Antelope Ground next to the Royal South Hants hospital and this would be the club's home for the best part of a decade. (see Antelope Ground)

In the close season of 1896, the committee entered into negotiations to purchase the ground outright, but they could not come to an agreement with the owners, with the result that the Antelope was sold to property developers and the club found itself homeless.

Help was at hand, however, and Hampshire CC offered the use of their backfield at the County Ground in Northlands Road at an annual rent of £200 per annum, however the club still had its sights on a ground it could call its own

There was a plan to move to the ground of the Club's early rivals and opponents in their first match Freemantle, but this fell through and things looked desperate until in 1898. Saints director George Thomas purchased some land only a few hundred yards from the County Ground. This was to become The Dell. (see The Dell)

After the War, as Saints fortunes soared there was talk of a move but nothing came of it. However in the 1970s there was talk was of a move to a new stadium on the site of the old power station and lido, incorporating a new shopping centre, hotel and leisure complex. Sadly it was only to be a political football kicked in anger in regard to these plans and amid inter-party wrangling, the plans were shelved.

By the early 90s Saints were again searching for a new home and a feasibility study identified 14 potential sites for a new stadium. Eventually these sites were narrowed down to one - old playing fields in Stoneham Lane in between Southampton & Eastleigh. The problem was that the land was owned by Hampshire County Council and fell under the jurisdiction of both Southampton and Eastleigh councils.

To get all three to agree on all points was nigh impossible and to cut a long story short, after over no less than seven years of argument, Stoneham was scrapped. In an initiative led by Southampton City Council plans were announced to keep Saints in the City at the old gasworks site in Northam, ironically at one of the original 14 sites identified in 1991.

And so Saints played their final league game at the Dell on Saturday May 19th. 2001 against Arsenal. Although the official closing was a week later with a friendly against Brighton with various other special events including a black tie dinner on the pitch and a supporters six a side tournament.

St Mary's was officially opened by Ted Bates on August 11th 2001, prior to a friendly match with Spanish side Espanyol, and it's been home to Saints ever since.

H
Half Time Turnarounds
In recent years Saints fans have been used to seeing other teams come from behind. Here are our top three second-half disasters when defeat has been snatched from the jaws of victory.

1. Tottenham Hotspur. (H) League. 16/04/79
After going in 3-0 up at the break, courtesy of a David Peach penalty, a goal from Alan Ball in his 600th league appearance, and a Phil Boyer goal, there couldn't have been a fan of either side who thought that Spurs would get a point. With half an hour left the score was still 3-0, however three goals in the next 20 minutes turned the game and when Spurs hit a post in the last minute Saints fans breathed a sigh of relief and took the point.

2. Tranmere Rovers.(A) FA Cup. 20/02/01
As Saints prepared to leave the Dell, they were going well under Glenn Hoddle and many thought that Saints name was written on the cup as they met Tranmere in the fifth round. However, the resolute Merseysiders had hung on for a scoreless draw at the Dell, to earn a replay. If the Rovers fans fancied their chances of a shock though, they were soon disappointed.

Hassan Kachloul scored on 11 and 25 minutes. When Dean Richards made it three on the stroke of half time, most thought the tie was all over, including Hoddle, who took off main scorer Pahars and brought on his countryman Bleidelis for a rare game.

Someone forgot to tell Tranmere, though for the first third of the second half, they failed to get a shot on target. Then it all changed. Ex-Saint Paul Rideout scored three times in 21 minutes and the visitors were on the rack. With seven minutes to go, Tranmere scored what would turn out to be the winner, prompting Pompey fans to deluge internet message boards with the joke, "What kind of house do Saints fans live in? Three up, four down!"

3. Leeds United. (H) League. 19/11/2005
When a goal from Marian Pahars and two from Nigel Quashie gave Saints a 3-0 lead at the break it looked like game over. For the first 25 minutes of the second half it seemed to be only a question of how many, as Saints missed chance after chance and Leeds rarely threatened.

But when they got their first with only 19 minutes to go,

the game turned drastically, and within 15 minutes they were leading 4-3 with Saints a shadow of their former selves.

Hagiology

The definition of Hagiology is:
1. Literature dealing with the lives of saints.
2. A collection of sacred writings.
3. An authoritative list of saints.

It was with this knowledge that Hagiology publishing was founded in 1998 by a group of Saints supporters. So far they have published five books, all of which are indispensable to any Southampton fan. *In that Number* is a statistical publication. *Full Time At The Dell* chronicles the former ground. *Match Of The Millennium* covers 100 matches of the 20th century, *Dell Diamond* is the biography of Ted Bates and *Saints v. Pompey* looks at our local derby. The sixth book will be a biography of Terry Paine.

Hitler Couldn't Stop 'Em

When Southampton played Plymouth Argyle in the final league game of 1938/39, two 20-year-olds Doug McGibbon and George Smith, had just broken into the side. For McGibbon the game was his debut. Both looked forward to the following season with enthusiasm, but they were not to know that the next league game would not to be for another seven years

When the league restarted in 1946, both were in the line-up to take on Swansea Town. McGibbon, a skilled air mechanic had spent much of the duration working on aircraft in Swindon. Smith for his part, served in the RAF as a rear gunner.

He was demobbed just in time to take his place in the Saints side. Nicknamed the "Guernsey Terrier" for his tenacious tackling, Smith made 101 appearances for Saints, scoring 1 goal. He retired from football in 1951 to emigrate to Australia where he remained till his death in 2001.

Nick Holmes (FA Cup Hero)

The unsung hero of the 1976 FA Cup Final side, Nick was the only Southampton born player in the final 12. Holmes made his debut at Arsenal in March 1974, aged only 19 and went on to enjoy a 13-year spell with the club.

Nick Holmes (right)

Nick also played in the 1979 League Cup Final at Wembley and scored what was arguably the goal of the game in the 2-3 defeat. Ironically the other goal for Saints was scored by the only other survivor of the 1976 Final, David Peach.

International honours sadly eluded Nick, although he was picked for an England U-23 squad only for injury to rule him out. He continued to be a regular in the Saints side until 1986. After starting the season with a testimonial game against Benfica, he soon picked up a pelvic injury that restricted his appearances and forced him to retire in May 1987. He spent a year with the club as a coach before leaving the game altogether to run a general store near Salisbury and then emigrating to Florida in 1999 for three years.

Since 2002 Holmes has managed Salisbury City, steadily steering them through the leagues, winning promotion to the Conference for season 2007/08, only one step from a return to league football for the one club man.
1974-87. 543 Apps. 64 goals.

I

Icebergs

There can't be too many football supporters who have had their week ruined by an Iceberg, but surely Southampton Football Club's can lay claim to that fact.

On the afternoon of Monday 8th April 1912, Saints

played host to Queens Park Rangers at the Dell. The crowd would probably have included a fair number of crew from the White Star lines new ship, RMS Titanic and were enjoying a last few days ashore before the start of the maiden voyage two days later.

They would have been pleased with the scoreless draw. After all, QPR were chasing the Southern League title. Sadly some of those who sailed on the Wednesday would not be there to see the outcome. Maybe they would have been pleased to have heard on the ship's radio that Saints had beaten Watford 2-1 at home on Saturday 13th April.

A day later football would be the last thing on anyone's minds as the ship hit an iceberg on Sunday 14th April at 23.40 hrs, sinking only two hours, forty minutes later. The ship's crew were made up mainly of Southampton men. Whilst the streets around St Mary's stadium are nowadays mainly industrial with post war housing, back in 1912 it was very different.

The area on which the ground now stands was hemmed in by street upon street of terraced houses. These were the districts where the men who made their living from the sea worked and lived. Both those who worked ashore as stevedores and those who went to sea.

The Chapel stand is named after the district that once stood behind it. Some of the Crew who lost their lives would have lived only yards from where the ground now stands. At the other end, Northam Estate is unrecognisable from the streets that once stood there. In 1912 the boundaries were clearly defined, you lived in Chapel or Northam, and the rivalry was intense.

St Mary's, despite the name of the present day stadium, is most definitely the other side of the railway track, as is the Church that gave both that district and the football club its name.

Individual Scoring Records

Most Goals In A Match (Pre War)
7 goals. Albert Brown. Southern League. v.

Northampton Town. (H) 28/12/01.
Brown scored seven in as Saints won 11-0. That season he scored 25 in 25 league games and four in the FA Cup, including the consolation goal in the 1-2 defeat against Sheffield United in the final at Crystal Palace.

Most Goals In a Match (Post War)
5 goals. Charlie Wayman. League Div 2. v. Leicester City. (H) 23/10/48.
Charlie had a great season, scoring 32 goals in 37 games, but his greatest haul was the five he bagged in the 6-0 drubbing of Leicester, Ted Bates scoring the other.

5 goals. Derek Reeves. League Cup v.Leeds United. (H) 05/12/60.
Perhaps the best remembered of the record scorers being that Reeves hit all five goals in the 5-4 beating of the Yorkshiremen in what is remembered as the longest game at the Dell.

Individual Goal Scorers - Season
25 goals. Matt Le Tissier. Premier. 1993/94.
37 goals. Ron Davies (pictured, left). Division 1. 1966-67.
32 goals. Charlie Wayman. Division 2. 1948/49
32 goals. George O'Brien. Division 2. 1964/65
39 goals. Derek Reeves. Division 3. 1959/60

Invasions
One sad aspect about the Premiership and all-ticket matches, with restricted away allocations, is that today's fans haven't experienced the excitement of going to an away match when the visiting supporters arrive like an invading army and take over the ground and the surrounding area, here are a few examples from Southampton's past!

Nottingham Forest 1963
This was a sixth round FA Cup replay and played at neutral White Hart Lane on a Monday evening in April 1963. Cup Fever had hit the City and an estimated 25,000 Saints fans were in the crowd of 42,256.

The invasion took everyone by surprise, including Spurs, who had not opened all the turnstiles. It meant that many fans didn't get in till half time. By then Saints were two up and would eventually win 5-0.

Leyton Orient 1966

This was the penultimate game of the 1965/66 season and with Saints needing a point to secure promotion (barring a mathematical catastrophe), some 12,000 Saints fans made Brisbane Road a virtual home game. With the point secured by a Terry Paine header, a massive pitch invasion saw the Saints players chaired off the pitch.

West Bromwich Albion 1976

As cup fever gripped the city, over 100 coaches and a special train were filled as Saints supporters headed en-masse for the West Midlands. They made up a third of the 36,634 crowd, mainly packed behind the Smethwick End goal

Luton Town/ Orient 1978

As Saints second promotion season to the top flight reached its climax, approximately 10,000 Saints supporters descended on the Bedfordshire town to cheer on their team.

As they entered Luton, they were surprised to see a similar convoy heading in the other direction, as local side Barton Rovers were playing in the FA Vase final at Wembley. Southampton's travelling fans made up the greater content of the 14,302, crowd. Three days later, Saints spookily found themselves in the same position as they had been a dozen years earlier, needing a point at Orient to virtually seal promotion. Again over 12,000 made the trip in another 19,000 crowd.

It was another header that secured the point, this time by Tony Funnell. Older Orient fans must have felt a sense of deja vu as the South Coast hordes poured onto the pitch at the final whistle, sadly injuring some of their on number as a wall collapsed.

Portsmouth 1984

It was the first South Coast derby for eight years as Saints travelled to Fratton Park for the FA Cup fourth round tie. Saints ticket allocation of 10,000, was swiftly

sold and with Saints fans also buying tickets in the home sections it was a 36,000 capacity crowd.

The visitors massed on the Milton Road terrace and on the terracing of one half of the South stand. With the game in injury time – added for treatment to Mark Dennis who'd been hit by a coin – the red half of Hampshire went barmy. Steve Moran's goal won the game for Saints.

Tottenham Hotspur 1989

Saints took their full allocation of 9,000 for this match, filling both the terraces and seats in the Park Lane end. They saw a great display of football as their team ripped Spurs apart.

Invincibles

In the late 19th century, the Southern League, was catching up fast with the rival Football League. FA Cup Final appearances by both Southampton and Tottenham Hotspur showed that the Southern League had come of age.

In 1896/97, Saints won the first of three Southern League titles in a row, winning 15 and drawing five of their 20-game programme.

To put this in perspective, in the 22 seasons since its inception in 1894 until most of its clubs, including Saints, joined the football league in 1920, only one other club achieved this feat – Millwall.

Ironically Millwall would have repeated their feat in the second season had they not been beaten 2-0 by Saints at the Antelope Ground in front of a then record 8,000 crowd.

During the ten-season period between 1896/97 and 1905/06, Saints won the Championship six times, were runners up once and third on the other three occasions. Add to that two FA Cup final appearances, one semi and a quarter final appearance.

It was true to say that Southampton were considered the greatest club south of Birmingham.

J

Japan

It may be a long way from Tokyo to Southampton, but on Sunday 7th October 2001, St Mary's hosted its first International game. The "home" club for the fixture weren't England but Japan, who took on Nigeria in a friendly. 11,801 spectators turned out in torrential rain to see the two sides draw two goals apiece.

Jehovah's Witnesses

For many years the Jehovah's Witnesses used to hold their annual South Of England convention at the Dell. Each summer, a stage was erected at the Archers Road end of the ground and thousands would descend to sit in the stands and listen to various delegates.
The final event was in June 2000.

The Dell, although not then demolished, was not available in 2001, as various farewell events were hosted exclusively by the football club at the Stadium. To date the conference hasn't been hosted at St Mary's.

Paul Jones

When Paul Jones arrived from Stockport to rejoin his former boss, namesake Dave, in the summer of 1997, eyebrows were raised by Saints supporters. At a time when the transfer budget was somewhat limited, they questioned how £900,000 been spent on a goalkeeper.

After all, Maik Taylor had been the hero of the previous season's relegation scrap and he was ably backed up by Neil Moss of whom great things were expected and Dave Beasant was also lurking in the background.

Paul Jones

Initially fans doubts seemed well-founded as Jones blundered his way through the first third of the season,. However two high-profile televised games against first Chelsea and then Manchester United were both won 1-0 with Jones magnificent. His form dropped in the final third of the season but he had done enough to be voted player of the year.

Jones would establish himself as Saints number one over the next five years, until the arrival of Antti Niemi. He seemed to be prone to error at times, but it has to be said that as a shot stopper he was second to none.

After the arrival of Niemi his chances were limited, but he played a big part in the 2003 FA Cup run, coming into the side for the semi final against Watford to replace the injured first choice man. Then he became the first goalkeeper to come on as a substitute in an FA Cup Final, after Niemi pulled a calf muscle in the 64th minute.

He also became, perhaps, the only keeper to lose a cup final without conceding a goal.

K

Kevin Keegan

Just as everyone knows where they were when they heard that John F Kennedy had been shot, every Southampton fan of a certain age knows just where they were when the news came through that the greatest player in Europe at that time, Kevin Keegan, had signed for Saints.

Keegan himself was at the Potters Heron Hotel at Ampfield one summer's day in 1980 . The Club had called a press conference there, but most journalists assumed it would be an announcement regarding a much-mooted new stadium. Lawrie McMenemy pulled off the coup of the season by revealing Keegan from behind the curtains.

To put it in perspective, Kevin was playing for Hamburg SV at the time. His last game for them would be the European Cup Final. (His last game for Liverpool had also been a European Cup final. Fans hoped this would be an omen.) He was the current European Footballer of the Year.

He stayed two seasons at Southampton, playing 80 games and scoring 42 goals. In his second season, 1981-82, Saints lead the League longer than any other club, but would ultimately fall short. What the fans didn't know, however, was that Keegan had fallen out with Lawrie McMenemy after a 0-3 home defeat to Aston Villa, and wanted away. It didn't prevent him being voted PFA player of the year that season.

There was a lot of bad feeling amongst supporters, as it was felt the news of Keegan's departure was kept secret till the season ticket deadline had passed.

However much the fans were disappointed in the manner of Keegan's departure, they remembered the good times he brought to the Dell. There hasn't been a time before or since when Saints have played such entertaining football or that has brought them so close to honours.

He will always be welcomed back to the club, by the fans at least, if not so much the car park attendant at the Dell.

A legend known as Jack, who when Keegan returned to commentate on a live game in the early 1990s and didn't have a pass, refused him entry with the old adage "I don't care if you are Kevin Keegan. No one gets in without a pass."
1980-82. 80 Apps. 42 goals.

Kit Manufacturers
Like many clubs, up until the 1970s Saints did not have a kit manufacturer. Team strips were supplied by local

Kevin Keegan

sports shop Toomers, who would presumably source the kit from various sources.

The team photo for the start of 1975/76 shows the side wearing shirts with the Umbro logo on, although the replica kits in the club shot weren't manufactured by the same company. Things were to soon change starting with the 1976 Cup Final.

May 1976- May 1980 - Admiral
Admiral produced the distinctive yellow kit for the Cup final and followed that up with a radical change in stripes for the Charity Shield, these two kits would last for four years with no change in design.

August 1980- May 1987-Patrick
With the arrival of Kevin Keegan and his deal with French company Patrick came a change in manufacturer and for seven years Saints remained loyal to the company even after the departure of Keegan. Their first design would remain unchanged for five years, their second for two.

August 1987- May 1991-Hummel
Saints started to see the commercial possibilities as they switched to Danish firm Hummel who dressed the team in what was basically the 1986 Danish World cup team design. They finally produced the first traditionally striped kit for 13 years, in 1989.

August 1991- May 1993-Admiral
A brief return to the Admiral fold. Bizarrely enough in their first season, Saints made a return to Wembley, meaning that all their appearances at the old stadium were in Admiral manufactured kits.

August 1993- May 1999-Pony
Pony were a big name in American football. Or so we were told when they attempted to gain a foothold in the UK sports market by producing kits for a number of

Premier clubs. Southampton's design for the first two years was appalling, although by 1995 they got their act together for perhaps the best kit of recent times.

August 1999- Present-Southampton FC
In 1999 Saints started to come into the calculator age and the mathematics were this. A replica shirt cost £40. Roughly speaking it cost £5 to make, £5 went to the manufacturer, £10 as a royalty to the club, with the remaining £20 being the profit for the retailer.

The big name manufacturers' first loyalty was to the big chain stores, meaning that when kits were launched the football club's shop received very few and the city centre sports shops the lions share. Saints, a club where few shirts were sold outside of the region took the bold step of manufacturing their own kits. With the coming of the internet age the time was right.

In truth its not rocket science, as not only do Saints make the shirts themselves but they only sell them through the club megastores.It means that instead of only earning £10 on the bulk of shirts sold, they can now make £35. The only real cost involved being the cost to make them.

(All costs involved are estimated from information supplied by the club in 1999.

Tony Knapp
Knapp is one of the forgotten heroes of Saints promotion side of 1966.

When he joined Saints from First Division Leicester in the summer of 1961, he was at the height of his powers and some would say on the verge of an England call-up. However manager Ted Bates was persuasive and forked out £27,500 to land the 24-year-old centre half. The fee was more than double the club's record outlay at the time.

It took Tony five years to get back in the top flight, but get back he did. He lead the team out in the club's first ever top flight fixture against Manchester City at the

Dell. That season he would make 39 league appearances, so it was a surprise when Saints let him go to newly promoted Coventry City in the summer of 1967. However Knapp was approaching 31and Ted Bates, as shrewd as ever, felt that the £20,000 fee was good business.

Tony Knapp

Knapp had a brief spell at Coventry before playing in the NASL for Los Angeles. He returned to England, joining Tranmere Rovers. He was player-manager at Poole Town and also managed the Iceland national side and Viking F.K. in Norway.
1961-67. 233 Apps. 2 goals.

L
Last Day Escapes
After the heady years of the 1980s, Saints started to spend more time at the wrong end of the table. It was a situation that continued into the 1990s. Southampton along with Coventry, got the reputation for being relegation escape experts.

This stereotyping was a little bit unfair. In 27 seasons in the top flight between 1977 and relegation in 2005, the club only went into the last day of the season with the threat of relegation hanging over their heads, four times.

1993/94
Saints travel to West Ham knowing that a win will be enough. Anything else and it's all about results elsewhere. Saints draw 3-3, but the other results go in their favour.

1995/96
Perhaps Saints closest ever scrape. Southampton, Coventry and Manchester City are all locked on 37 points. The third and final relegation spot is ready and

waiting for one of them. Saints have a far better goal difference than Man City, so a win will be enough. Anything less and it could be curtains.

Saints play out a nervy goalless draw at home to Wimbledon. It looks good, though, as Manchester City are two down at home to Liverpool. But then they pull back to 2-2. Ex-Saints boss, Alan Ball, in charge at City, somehow gets the message that Saints have gone a goal down.

He orders his side to keep the ball, thinking they don't need a winner. But they do. All three sides draw and its Manchester City who go down.

1998/99
Saints beat Everton 2-0 at the Dell to complete a miraculous turn around over the season. (See Great Escape).

Matthew Le Tissier

All football clubs have a select group players considered to be a cut above anyone else. Since the war, Saints have been blessed with more than their fair share of such legends. None has been worshipped more than Matthew Paul Le Tissier.

The man who would be known simply as Le God first came to the attention of Southampton when he toured Hampshire with a Guernsey under-15 side. He joined the club as an apprentice in the summer of 1985. It wasn't long before he made his first team debut as a substitute at Norwich City on the 30th August 1986. This was followed a few days later by his full debut at home to his boyhood idols, Tottenham Hotspur.

Supporters got the first taste of his genius though, when he came off the bench against Manchester United in the League Cup. He scored two goals to sink the Red Devils and left Ron Atkinson cursing, as he was sacked on the back of the defeat. It was clear that Saints had a talent on their books.

Le Tissier continued to hit the net and finished the season as a regular in the side. The following season

Matthew Le Tissier

was one of learning for the Channel Islander as he battled to make his mark.

The next season, 1988/89, he broke through with a vengeance. He consolidated in 1989/90 to such a degree that there were some that said that he should go to Italy for the World Cup.

Strangely, Matt never won an England U-21 cap, although he would win England B honours. It would be March 1994 before he won the first of his eight full

England caps, despite being mentioned as a possibility, or probability, for just about every England squad announced.

With the arrival of Ian Branfoot as manager, critics pondered whether the new manager's long-ball style would suit Matt. Publicly Branfoot always said the right things about the player, but to the fans it was clear that the manager wanted brawn and not brain and Le Tissier came very close to joining Spurs.

The arrival of Alan Ball as manager sparked Le Tissier's golden period at the Dell. Scoring spectacular goal after goal, he seemingly kept Saints in the top flight single-handed. As the 1998 World Cup loomed, Le Tissier's hopes of playing in it dimmed. England manager Glenn Hoddle discarded him after a qualifier defeat against Italy.

Matt continued to do his talking where it mattered, on the pitch. He hit 16 goals in 38 games in 1996/97, and when he ran out at Loftus Road in April 1998 for an England B game against Russia, he was in fine form.

He scored a hat-trick, and the consensus was that Hoddle would take him to France. He didn't, and since then there has been the niggling feeling that Matt was never quite the same player again. He knew that at 30, he wouldn't have another chance to play in a major tournament.

Over the next three seasons, Le Tissier would be ravaged by injury. He had never been the greatest athlete and now his body seemed to resist the rigours of modern day training methods. By the time of the last home game of the 2000-01season, Le God had started only two league games. He had made five sporadic appearances as substitute and his last start was in October. It was felt that he was only on the bench for sentimental reasons.

In May 2001, Arsenal were the opposition for the last ever league game at the Dell. With 16 minutes left to play and the score locked at 2-2, Le Tissier came on to a great roar. He didn't look fit and the chance to score seemed to have gone. The referee checked his watch. The players nervously eyed the crowd, who were preparing to invade the pitch at the sound of the final whistle. Then it happened. The ball dropped to Matt on the edge of the area. He swivelled and hit it with his left foot in one movement. It seemed to go in slow-motion. The crowd erupted. It was one of the greatest moments at the Dell, from one of the greatest players, in the final minute. You couldn't have written that script if you tried.

The following season Matt made only four appearances as a substitute. Everyone knew it was all over. The player had done more than anyone to ensure that Saints stayed in the Premier League. But the new stadium, built on the back of that status, would never witness a Le Tissier goal.

In the final game of the 2001-02 season against Newcastle United, Gordon Strachan put him on the bench. Any chance he had of a second fairytale, though, came to an end when El Khalej was sent off for a foul. Saints were winning 2-1 at the time and Strachan, knowing that a draw would see them slip five places, not to mention lose something like £1.5 million in prize money, had to be cautious. Le Tissier was obliged to remain rooted to his seat on the bench.

The legendary career had ended. The fans stood on their seats and applauded him till their hands were raw, such was their love for him.

There are supporters who would claim that Terry Paine or Mick Channon could rival Matt for Southampton fans' affection. One thing is for certain, though. Neither of them had a record dedicated to them or a pub named after them. Or, as happened in February 2007, had a plane named after them.

Saints sponsor Flybe.com did exactly that, and put a picture on the fuselage of Le God celebrating a goal in the 6-3 thrashing of Manchester United in 1996. Now that's taking adoration to new heights.

1986-2002. 463 (78) Apps. 210 goals.

Longest Game

What is generally regarded as the longest ever game played at the Dell, was also one of the most pulsating games ever seen at the ground.

On December 5th 1960, Leeds United were the visitors in the 4th round of the inaugural season of the League cup. The time table went like this:

7.30pm. Kick off
7.40pm. Floodlights go out as Leeds are taking a throw in.
7.57pm. After standing bemused on the pitch, the players return to dressing room as the crowd are informed that electricians are working on the fault.
8.09pm. Lights are back on at two-thirds power. Game resumes.
8.15 pm. Derek Reeves puts Saints 1-0 up with header.
8.20pm. Jones of Leeds is being treated on the touchline when Ron Reynolds the Saints keeper, is injured. As he is being treated the lights go out again. Reynolds is stretchered off in pitch darkness. Jones limps off.
8.54pm. Lights back on with full power. Saints are down to ten men with Cliff Huxford in goal.
8.57pm. Reeves puts Saints 2-0 up.
9.05pm. Reeves completes his hat trick. 3-0 Saints.
9.17pm. Half time
9.25pm. Second half starts. Both sides now have only ten men as the injured Jones fails to appear.
9.28pm. Reeves nets his fourth of the night.
9.32pm. Peyton is in place to pull one back for Leeds 4-1.
9.42pm. McCole for the visitors, makes the score 4-2.
9.48pm. Jack Charlton scores for Leeds. Saints now have only a slender lead, 4-3.
9.58pm. Cameron scores a penalty for Leeds to level the tie 4-4.
10.09 pm. With only 25 seconds left, Derek Reeves scores his fifth to win the tie.
10.10pm. Referee G.W. Thorpe blows for full time.

Rupert Lowe

Most Saints fans would be hard pushed to name three chairmen of Southampton Football Club. However, there is one man who every supporter would be able to name and that is Rupert Lowe.

In the mid-1990s, the Saints board were planning to float the club on the London Stock Exchange. Finding it to be a long and costly procedure, they chose instead, a reverse takeover. They needed to find a company that had already floated and take it over, while effectively being taken over themselves. Lowe's company Secure Retirements, was a perfect candidate. After the deal, Lowe became chairman of the football club.

Lowe's previous claim to fame was that he had stood for Parliament as a candidate for the UK Independence party and he arrived at the club on the back of a motorbike bringing with him several of his old school chums from Radley Public school as board members.

Initial reaction from the fans to Lowe was not favourable to put it mildly. When Graeme Souness and Lawrie McMenemy walked out, allegedly because they couldn't work with him, things seemed to be in dire straits.

Lowe, however, rode his luck as first David Jones and then Glenn Hoddle stabilised the club on the playing side. Hoddle's subsequent departure to Tottenham, however, was an unfortunate and messy affair. The appointment of Stuart Gray as Hoddle's successor proved short-lived.

Gray was quickly dismissed and Lowe brought in Gordon Strachan. If the fans had been rebelling a few years earlier they were positively anarchic now. Strachan had just overseen the relegation of Coventry City. Perhaps the Scotsman felt that being public enemy number two in Southampton was better than his standing in the midlands city.

Then it all started to go right for the club. Lowe was the hero of Southampton. Saints enjoyed comfortable mid-table placings under Strachan, along with an FA Cup Final appearance and a UEFA Cup campaign. But the problem was that Lowe appeared to be letting his ego run away with itself. He gave the impression that he knew more about football than those who'd been in the game for decades. After Strachan left, it was one disastrous managerial appointment after another.

First Paul Sturrock arrived and departed. Then it was déjà vu all over again, as Steve Wigley, like Gray four years earlier, was promoted to the manager's job. He was sacked before the paint had dried on the door.

Lowe now tried his fourth manager in less than a year. The appointment of Harry Redknapp and then relegation, were the final nails in Lowe's coffin

Every game would see protests against him and finally an EGM was called by a consortium of shareholders. Lowe accepted that he couldn't remain and stood down in July 2006, after nine years at the helm.

Lowe like many leaders, ultimately failed because he started to believe he was infallible. He failed to learn from the mistakes he had made.

In terms of business, he ran Saints as a tight ship and it has to be said that he took Saints from the 19th century Dell to the 21st century St Mary's.

The supporters judge him though, on his record of overseeing Southampton's relegation from the Premier League after 27 years in the top division.

Lucky Seven

If one shirt is considered to be the shirt of the gods then Southampton Football Club reveres the number seven.

It started with Terry Paine, in the days before squad numbers. Terry Paine would more often than not wear

the lucky seven and its fair to say he wore it more times than anyone else in a playing career lasting over 17 years.

When Paine left the club in 1974 it was passed around a little bit. Paul Gilchrist being the man who wore it at Wembley in 1976. From the following season a certain Alan James Ball wore it with distinction including in the 1979 League Cup Final at Wembley.

In 1980 the most famous number seven in the world took receipt of the jersey. Kevin Keegan of course, and although he would only wear it for two seasons, what a pair of seasons they were.

Then for a few seasons the shirt was in limbo, mainly being worn by Nick Holmes. As Holmes retired a new man stepped forward to take possession.

He arguably produced some of the greatest performances seen in that number. The man known was simply as Le God. Whenever Southampton scored a great goal between 1987 and 2001, then invariably the scorer had the number seven on his back.

The season following Le Tissier's retirement, no one was allocated the number. Then in 2003 Kevin Phillips arrived and it was felt that he was high profile enough to wear the prized number seven on his back.

In 2006 Rudi Skacel arrived from Hearts with a reputation that hinted that he could just be the next great player to wear the number.

In his first season he didn't quite live up to the hype, but then again Saints fans over the past five decades have demanded and got high standards from the wearer. When they sing " I want to be in that number" make no mistake about what that number is: seven.

M
Man About The House

ITV sitcom "Man About The House" was first aired in 1973. It starred Richard O'Sullivan, Paula Wilcox and Sally Thomsett. It was the story of a young man, Robin Tripp, sharing a flat with two girls Chrissy and Jo. Not a big thing in today's enlightened world, but back then many saw it as the final nail in the coffin of the British Empire. A man living in the same flat as two girls, un-chaperoned? Whatever next.

Although the series was set in Earls Court, our hero Robin is from Southampton and is often to be heard espousing the merits of the football team.

Sally Thomsett, Richard O'Brien and Paula Wilcox in Man About The House

In an episode in the first series entitled Match of the Day, Robin takes the girls to watch a cup tie at The Dell between Saints and Arsenal.

The girls only go because they fancy Charlie George. Robin's car breaks down en-route and he is nearly beaten up by some Arsenal supporters, only getting saved by Chrissy and Jo fluttering their eyelids at them. The girls then disappear into the distance, and sadly for Robin he misses the match and Saints lose. The Gunners fans and the girls pass him on their way home. It's not always easy being a Saints fan.

Managers - Post War
Bill Dodgin. Jan 1946-August 1949.
Joined the club as a player in 1939, but the War meant that he only made four official peacetime appearances for Saints, all in the FA Cup. He was Saints manager for the first post war League season and almost guided Saints into the top flight in the last two of his three seasons, before being tempted to manage Fulham.

Sydney Cann. August 1949- December 1951.
As a player, Cann appeared in the 1933 Cup Final with Manchester City. Syd had joined Saints as the physio after the war and following the departure of Dodgin, on the eve of the 1949 season, he stepped into the breach. In his first season took Saints to within a hairs breadth of promotion, missing out on goal average. But the club was already in decline and in December 1951 he stood down due to a difference of opinion with the board.

Committee. December 1951-March 1952.
In those days they didn't rush things. After the departure of Cann, the team was selected by a committee of directors, coaching staff and to complicate matters further, three players - Mallett, Clements and Horton.

George Roughton. March 1952- September 1955.
Roughton was manager of Exeter City when Saints appointed him, but he was stepping into a cauldron. In his first full season Saints were relegated for the first

time in their history. After going close to getting the side back up at the second attempt, Roughton resigned due to health reasons.

Ted Bates. September 1955-November 1973. (see also Ted Bates)
When Roughton resigned several games into the 1955/56 season the club didn't have to look too far when they appointed reserve team coach Ted Bates. They couldn't have known what an inspirational appointment this would be. He built up the club to become a real force. It wasn't an overnight success, more a gradual progression. Southampton would not achieve promotion till his fifth season in charge, but solid long term foundations, on and off the field were being built.

Lawrie McMenemy. November 1973-June 1985. (See also Lawrie McMenemy)
The big Geordie arrived at the club in the summer of 1973 with the official title of Team Manager Designate. The idea was that Bates would ease McMenemy into the job. On November 15th with Saints in the top ten, it was thought it was time to make the change. However all would not go to plan and the team careered towards relegation. Luckily the board backed him despite the supporters' demands and the next decade would be the greatest in the club's history.

Chris Nicholl. June 1985-June 1991.
Former player Chris Nicholl returned to the Club after two years learning his trade as assistant manager at Grimsby Town. Perhaps the directors thought that this was a good omen as McMenemy had arrived from the same club 12 years earlier. Whatever the reasons, McMenemy would obviously be a hard act to follow, especially since football was changing as it headed towards the Premiership.

Chris Nicholl

The fans were dismayed that Nicholl seemed to be a lot more cautious than his predecessor. This was no bad thing in the circumstances and in his first season Nicholl lead Saints to an FA Cup Semi Final. He followed this with a League Cup semi in his second year. No mean feat, as Nicholl had to oversee a change of the guard. A few older players left or retired, whilst he bedded-in new boys from an exceptional crop of youngsters.

In the summer of 1991, despite the fact that Saints had good runs in both cups and were only four points off a second consecutive top 10 finish, the directors sensed that both the players and the crowd didn't have the faith in the manager. They sensationally sacked him, the first manager in the Clubs history to suffer this fate.

Ian Branfoot. June 1991-January 1994.
Having a reputation as a "long ball merchant," Branfoot immediately assured the crowd that they would be watching entertaining football. However getting rid of Jimmy Case was not going to do his standing any good and it soon became clear that Saints were turning from an exciting footballing side into a team that relied on stopping the opposition playing and hoofing it long. The manager tried to tell the fans different but they all knew their eyes weren't deceiving them. After two consecutive relegation dog fights, Saints were halfway through a third when the board caved in to supporters protests and sacked perhaps the most reviled man in Saints history.

Alan Ball. January 1994-July 1995.
The arrival of Alan Ball from Exeter City was a breath of fresh air. The style of play immediately changed, as Ball based his entire tactics on giving the ball to Matt Le Tissier. He dragged the team out of a relegation fight and in his second season took the team to 10th,

Alan Ball

but just as things were looking up, in came Manchester City with a job offer. Ball claimed Saints didn't do enough to keep him, but that didn't wash with the supporters, who celebrated at the end of the following season as City went down and Saints stayed up.

Dave Merrington. July 1995-June 1996.
Dave Merrington had been a coach at the club since 1984 and was responsible for the development of a host of great Saints players. It was always going to be a hard job to step up to management, especially since the transfer budget was non existent, but Merrington managed it. Against all the odds he kept Saints up on the final day of the season, hiding the fact that his wife was seriously ill. His reward was to be sacked a month later – perhaps the most despicable act ever perpetuated by the board of the club.

Graeme Souness. July 1996-May 1997.
Great things were expected from the appointment of Souness and initially things looked great. A plethora of

signings, followed by a couple of great wins put the club in mid- table. However it was a long hard winter and Saints still endured a final day nerve-wracker to stay up. With new Chairman, Rupert Lowe now in charge, Souness became unhappy with the situation and resigned.

Dave Jones. June 1997-January 2000.
Jones arrived after his Stockport County side had knocked Saints out of the League Cup the previous season. In his first season he seemed to tinker too much with the side, bringing in lower league players who weren't up to the job, although a good run mid-season meant and a 12th place finish was a fair showing. His second season was a disaster from the start. By Christmas, Saints looked set for the drop. However a great late run which became known as the "Great Escape," dragged Saints clear.

Dave Jones

In the summer, Jones was hit by allegations relating to his former job as a care worker. Rupert Lowe gave Jones gardening leave to fight the upcoming court case. The allegations would prove to be totally unfounded and false. The judge recorded a not guilty verdict and commented that the case should have never reached the trial stage.

Having already installed Glenn Hoddle as a stand-in manager, Southampton paid off the remainder of Jones' contract. Jones contended that this amounted to unfair dismissal and he took the case to an industrial tribunal, but the decision was upheld.

Glenn Hoddle. January 2000-March 2001.
Hoddle was initially given a temporary appointment while Dave Jones fought his court case, but in October 2000 he was given an 18-month contract. Hoddle was a breath of fresh air and soon introduced a system of football not seen since the McMenemy days. However

Glenn Hoddle

his good work had not gone unnoticed at other clubs. He was lured to Tottenham Hotspur mid-season, to the anger of Saints supporters. He was promptly installed as public enemy number one, amid allegations of underhand dealings. Revenge was gleaned when Saints beat Spurs 3-1 at White Hart Lane in September 2003 and Hoddle was promptly sacked.

Stuart Gray. March 2001-October 2001.
Initially appointed as caretaker to see Saints through to the end of the season. No one expected the position to be made permanent, especially with a record of Won Two, Drawn Two, Lost Five. The two wins were the very last games at The Dell when two under strength Manchester United and Arsenal sides were beaten. After eight games of the next season Southampton had won two and lost six, with a defeat at West Ham dropping the club to second bottom. The newspapers made much of Gordon Strachan attending the game,

suggesting that he would replace the incumbent manager.

Gordon Strachan. October 2001-March 2004.
At the start, the appointment of Gordon Strachan was regarded with caution. He had only recently been in

Gordon Strachan

charge of Coventry City's relegation from the top division. Within six months, however, he had become "Wee Gordon Strachan" to the faithful. In his second season he took Saints to the FA Cup Final. There was a sense that after that he was at odds with the chairman over transfer policy and it was no surprise when he left the club in March 2004. However no one could have predicted the events that would follow

Paul Sturrock. March 2004-August 2004.
Sturrock arrived from Plymouth Argyle and it was hoped that he would take the club up a step from the foundations built by Strachan. However if rumours could be believed, all was not well on the training ground. Several senior players apparently found his methods primitive to say the least and only two games into the new season he parted company, by "mutual consent."

Steve Wigley. August 2004-December 2004.
Wigley had been briefly caretaker boss after the departure of Strachan and had stated then that he had no desire to be a Premiership manager. So it was a shock when it was announced he was the new boss on a permanent basis. Many thought that Wigley was just a front for Lowe's determination to get former England Rugby coach Sir Clive Woodward involved with management. After only 14 games, Wigley was sacked.

Harry Redknapp. December 2004-December 2005.
The revolving door spun again and Harry Redknapp was the unlikely new arrival – the club's fourth manager in one calendar year. Redknapp had been

boss at Portsmouth until only a few weeks earlier, and claimed he wanted a break from the game, although it was common knowledge that he had fallen out with the Pompey chairman. Saints fans revelled in the TV images of crying Pompey fans as they begged him not to leave and then laughed as he was denounced as Judas. However the last laugh was on Saints as Redknapp failed to halt the slump. The club were relegated after 27 years in the top division. Harry Redknapp left to return to Portsmouth a week short of a year in charge at St Mary's.

George Burley. December 2005-Present.
Burley faced a difficult task as the remains of Saints Premier League side left and he started the rebuilding process to challenge for promotion. In his first full season, Saints made the play-offs only to be knocked out by Derby County on penalties.

Manchester United Rivalry

Manchester United always seem to crop up at key moments in Southampton's history. The clubs met for the first time as long ago as 1896/97 in the FA Cup. United were then known as Newton Heath. A crowd of 8,000 turned up to see the Lancashire side earn a one-all draw at the County ground, which was a good 1,000 more than saw the Saints defeated 1-3 in the replay up north.

In the 1976 FA Cup Final Saints had the audacity to prevent United winning their first trophy in years. It suddenly became personal for them as well as Saints. Of course they had their revenge the following season.

In the mid Eighties Saints beat United 4-1 in the Littlewoods cup at the Dell and a youngster called Le Tissier hit the headlines scoring twice, its fair to say he wasn't on Ron Atkinson's Christmas card list as the Old Trafford manager got the sack the following day.

The general tone had been set. The fixture was always a bit of a grudge match for Saints, and the feeling was to some extent, mutual. It would be never be in the same bracket for United as a derby game with City or a contest with Liverpool, but there were always enough

little incidents to incur the wrath of their fans and manager. Beating Saints meant a little bit more to them than they would like to admit. In short, little old Southampton managed to spring up and humiliate them at frequent intervals.

Perhaps the most remembered occasion was the "Grey Shirts" incident in April 1996 at the Dell. A relegation threatened Saints met a title chasing Salford side, wearing their "trendy" grey change strip. The home side raced to a remarkable 3-0 half time lead. As the teams ran out for the second half something was different, United were in blue, not grey. Sir Alex Ferguson, then just plain Fergie, raged that his players had found it difficult to pick out each other against the crowd. That should have been easy. Saints fans were the ones standing up, shouting lewd songs about Posh Spice. The change of shirts did not change much. United got a goal back but it wasn't enough.

The following season Fergie swore that his side would be the ones scoring three this time. Spookily he was right, but he hadn't reckoned on Saints hitting six. At half time United were 3-1 down. Fifteen thousand southerners sang "Are you going to change your shirts?" It's unlikely Sir Alex saw the funny side of the chant, and the thousand Southerners in the away section weren't laughing either.

If Manchester United could just about take Saints humiliating them at The Dell, it was a different matter in their own backyard. So when Saints arrived at Old Trafford in September 1999, the usual slaughter was anticipated.

However Masimo Taibi, the United goalkeeper must have been a closet Saints fan as he dived over a miss-hit Le Tissier 25-yard trickler, blaming his studs in the process. Once again the whole country was laughing at United and Saints got a rare point a the Theatre of Errors.

But as Fergie and his cohorts know, what goes around comes around, and it would be Manchester United who would send Saints out of the Premiership. Despite his penchant for playing virtual reserve sides in meaningless end of season fixtures, Sir Alex put out the strongest side he could, for the final day of the 2004-05 season. Southampton had to win the game and hopes were raised when John O'Shea put through his own goal.

But a first half Darren Fletcher equaliser and a winner from Ruud Van Nistelrooy saw Saints tumble out of the top flight. When Roy Keane taunted distraught Saints supporters in the stadium as he warmed down after the end of the game, it didn't go down too well either.

The rivalry is far from concluded, merely on pause. Although the younger generation of Manchester Unexcited fans barely remember even the grey shirt incident, older supporters will know there is something special when the two clubs meet. Until the next time…

Jim McCalliog (centre) with Mick Channon and Peter Osgood

Jim McCalliog (FA Cup Hero)

When Saints signed the Scottish international from Manchester United in February 1975, it seemed he was a lot older than his 28 years. Possibly this was because he had been the most expensive teenager back in the 1960s.

McCalliog was also not the most popular man in Southampton on his arrival. He was regarded as the man who had sent Saints down nine moths earlier when he scored a penalty to earn United a draw at the Dell. That extra point would have seen Saints safe. However he soon became a mainstay of the side, barely missing a game up until the FA Cup final.

Jim played a bigger part in the cup run than many remember. It was his brace that sent Saints to victory in the third round replay at Villa Park. He followed that up with a sweetly struck free kick in the quarter final at Bradford City and of course it was his pin point pass that send Bobby Stokes scurrying through at Wembley for that winning goal.

He stayed a further season at Saints before departing to the States to play for Chicago Sting. He now runs a pub in Wetherby, West Yorkshire.
1975-77. 88 (2) Apps. 8 goals.

Lawrie McMenemy

After taking over from Ted Bates and taking the club to a fifth place finish in the League, McMenemy was dismayed as the club plummeted towards relegation. In 1974, they became the first victims of the three up three down rule change.

In his second season in charge many expected an instant return to the top flight and when this was not forthcoming turned on McMenemy. To his credit the former Guardsman never baulked at the 50-yard walk from the tunnel to the dug out. In his second full season, Saints would again fail in the promotion stakes but would win the FA Cup. The big Geordie was a hero not just in Hampshire but nationwide due to his TV work and of course, who could forget his Barbican advert with the catchphrase: "It's great, man."

He rebuilt the side several times and although Saints would never reach the heights of May 1976 again, the McMenemy years were a golden era, with cup runs and even a runners-up spot to the invincible Liverpool side of the 1980's, the highlights.

But rumours had always abounded of bigger clubs wanting Lawrie and in the summer of 1985 he was finally tempted. The surprise was that it was Sunderland, not just because he was from Newcastle, their biggest rivals, but because they had just been relegated to the Second Division. It was surely a step down from the Saints who had finished the previous season fifth.

True to his word though, he did get them out of the Second Division, or he would have done, if he hadn't resigned just a month before they dropped into the Third for the first time in their history, in 1987. Even today he is a hated man on Wearside prompting the joke, "What have Lawrie McMenemy and the Titanic got in common? They both should never have left Southampton!"

Lawrie McMenemy celebrates after leading Saints to victory in the FA Cup semi-final in 1976

But unlike the ship, a return to Southampton happened in December 1993, when Lawrie was appointed director of football at The Dell. However he apparently fell out with chairman Rupert Lowe and left in the summer of 1997 along with Graeme Souness.

The bitterness with Lowe meant that in the next nine years he rarely returned to watch the team play, despite continuing to live in the area. Nevertheless, it was clear from his newspaper articles and broadcasting work that Saints were his first love .

Some Saints fans feel that McMenemy, having left the club twice, should remain in the history books, but that would be harsh on a man who has done more for the club than anyone else apart from Ted Bates.

This was recognised by the new board of directors who, on ousting Rupert Lowe in the summer of 2006, immediately invited Lawrie to join the footballing board of the Club.

The Milton Mob

In the 1960s, the vocal exhortations of Liverpool's Kop spurred on every team to have its own version of a football choir. Saints vocal element gathered at the Milton Road End of The Dell behind the goal. They went under the banner of the Milton Mob, with their legendary leader Dougal.

Sadly the one drawback of the Dell at the time was that both ends were open so they couldn't achieve the decibels reached at other grounds with covered terraces.

For the best part of a decade, the Milton Mob ruled The Dell, then in the mid 1970s things started to change. The boot boy element migrated to the Archers Road end to taunt the away supporters, whilst some started to stand under the west stand where they felt that the roof offered a louder sound.

The last true season for the Milton Mob was 1976/77. The following year, that part of the terracing was fenced off and designated the Family Centre, however it did enjoy a swansong in the late 1980s when a younger element, dubbed the Milton Muppets by other sections of the support, appeared.

The rest deemed themselves too cool to wear replica shirts, but once again The Milton Road End lead the singing at The Dell.

N

Names

What do Holland and Southampton have in common? Answer: Neither of them have Hills! While Hill is a common surname in football, Saints have never had a player with that surname at any time in their history.

•••

"There's only one Ron Davies" sang the Milton Road choir in the late 1960s but they had short memories. This was because free-scoring centre forward Ronald Tudor Davies, the subject of their affections, was actually the second RT Davies to wear the striped shirt.

Fellow Welshman, Ronald Thomas Davies played 192 times between 1957-64. Unlike his namesake, he hadn't a clue where the net was and failed to score even once. In fairness, though, he was a full back. (see Ron Davies)

•••

Traditionally, football clubs scoured coal mines to search for talent. In 1974, however, Southampton appeared to be basing their scouting activities around the House of Lords.

Two Earls turned out for the side, at that time. Mick Earls made eight appearances for the club, although he sadly never got to Lord it in the same side as Pat Earles, who played 18 times scoring 2 goals, including one game in the 1976 FA Cup run.

•••

Perhaps one of the shortest Saints careers was that of Marco Almeida whose club career consisted of 11 minutes against Arsenal in 1999. But the name on the shirt told only part of the story. He had perhaps one of the longest monikers in club history.

His full title was Antonio Bernado Parcana Marco Almeida. At 33 letters, it was three more than Emmanuel Franciszek Andruszewski, who himself dwarfed the exotically entitled Reuben Omojola Folasanje Agboola. All together now, "There's only one Reuben Omajola…" If only Ali Dia had scored that day.

Nearly Men

Saints have always enjoyed a prolific youth system and over the years it provided not only a plethora of Saints stars but a king's ransom in transfer fees. However, sometimes they got it wrong and here is a list of players who slipped through the system and were released, only to find fame and fortune elsewhere.

Steve Foster

An associate schoolboy, Foster was turned down for an apprenticeship. Taken on by Pompey, he enjoyed a great career with Brighton, Aston Villa and Luton Town amongst others.

Kevin Phillips

Failed to earn a professional contract at The Dell, although in fairness he was playing as a full back. He was spotted playing for Baldock by Watford and then went to Sunderland, where he enjoyed the best spell of his career before joining Saints for a couple of seasons.

Graham Roberts

After failing to get taken on as an apprentice, Southampton-born Roberts drifted into non- league football, where he was spotted playing for Weymouth by Tottenham Hotspur. He won FA Cup Winner's medals and then League titles at Glasgow Rangers before falling out with future Saints boss Graeme Souness. Spells at Chelsea and WBA followed.

Sir Bobby Robson

Not a lot of people know that future England boss Bobby Robson was on Saints books as an amateur in 1949. However, he wasn't taken on professionally and the rest as they say is history.He enjoyed a long and distinguished career at both club and international level. Did we mention that the England Italia 90 semi-final was first planned in a boarding house in Hill Lane? Erm, no. Even we wouldn't claim that one.

Lawrie Sanchez

Another who was turned down for an apprenticeship only to enjoy great success. While with Wimbledon he won an FA Cup winners medal in 1988 and since then has had a successful career as a club and national team manager.

Dennis Wise

Arguably, the biggest fish to get away. He was offered a professional contract but fell out with then manager Lawrie McMenemy who, after Wise agreed to sign, withdrew the offer at the eleventh hour. Glory with Wimbledon, Chelsea and England followed.

Neutral Venues

Saints have played many games at neutral venues over the years. This list includes all FA Cup semi finals. Ordered by highest attendance.

Wembley. 01/05/1976 *FA Cup Final v. Manchester United.* won 1-0 100,000

Wembley. 17/03/1979 *League Cup Final v. Nottingham Forest.* lost 2-3 100,000

Wembley. 14/08/1976 *Charity Shield v. Liverpool.* lost 0-1 76,500

The Crystal Palace. 21/04/1900 *FA Cup Final v. Bury.* lost 0-4 75,000

The Crystal Palace. 19/04/1902 *FA Cup Final v. Sheffield United.* drew 1-1 74,479

Millennium Stadium. 17/05/2003 *FA Cup Final v. Arsenal.* lost 0-1 73,726

Villa Park. 27/04/1963 *FA Cup Semi Final v. Manchester United.* lost 0-1 68,312

Wembley. 29/03/1992 *Zenith Data Systems Cup Final v. Nottingham Forest.* lost 2-3 67,688

Stamford Bridge. 28/03/1925 *FA Cup Semi Final v. Sheffield United.* lost 0-2 65,754

Stamford Bridge. 03/04/1976 *FA Cup Semi Final v. Crystal Palace.* won 2-0 52,810

Stamford Bridge. 26/03/1927 *FA Cup Semi Final v. Arsenal.* lost 1-2 52,133

Highbury. 14/04/1984 *FA Cup Semi Final v. Everton.* lost 0-1 46,587

Stamford Bridge. 28/03/1908 *FA Cup Semi Final v. Wolverhampton Wanderers.* lost 0-2 45,000

White Hart Lane. 05/04/1986 *FA Cup Semi Final v. Liverpool.* lost 0-2 44,605

Villa Park. 13/04/2003 *FA Cup Semi Final v. Watford.* won 2-1 42,602

White Hart Lane. 08/04/1963 *FA Cup 6th Round 2nd Replay v. Nottingham Forest.* won 5-0 42,256

The Crystal Palace. 28/04/1902 *FA Cup Final Replay v. Sheffield United.* lost 1-2 40,000

The Crystal Palace. 24/03/1900 *FA Cup Semi Final v. Millwall.* drew 0-0 30,000

White Hart Lane. 15/03/1902 *FA Cup Semi Final v. Nottingham Forest.* won 3-1 30,000

Bramall Lane. 19/03/1898 *FA Cup Semi Final v. Nottingham Forest.* drew 1-1 30,000

The Crystal Palace. 23/03/1898 *FA Cup Semi Final Replay v. Nottingham Forest.* lost 0-2 12,000

Elm Park. 15/03/1900 *FA Cup Semi Final Replay v. Millwall.* won 3-0 12,000

Chris Nicholl

Signed for £80,000 by Lawrie McMenemy at the start of 1977/78 season, Nicholl was a big central stopper who wasn't afraid to get hurt. He was seen as just the man to put the bite into Saints promotion challenge, although when he joined he was about to turn 31. Few expected him to be around for long. How wrong they were.

Chris had been a late starter in League football, before enjoying five years at Aston Villa. He captained their 1977 League Cup winning side, scoring a glorious 40-yard goal in the process. His other claim to fame was scoring all four goals in a 2-2 draw with Leicester in 1976, all from open play.

Chris Nicholl

In his first season at The Dell, he missed just three games as he lead the side back to the top flight. He continued to feature through some of the greatest years the club has known. Most remarkably, he was ever-present in his final season as a player at Southampton, in 1982/83, at the age of 36.

A quietly spoken man off the field who always had time for the supporters, he is remembered with great fondness both as player and manager. (see Managers) 1977-83. 268 Apps. 9 goals.

Nicknames

Psycho - Mark Dennis (For obvious reasons)
Le God - Matt Le Tissier (He was worshipped)
Harpo - Eric Martin (His hair resembled Harpo Marx)
Elvis - Terry Paine (In early days he would take a guitar on away trips and he grew Elvis sideburns)
Spike - David Armstrong (Irony at its best)
Fusey - Micky Adams (He was known to have a short fuse)
Killer - Michael Svensson (For his no nonsense approach)
The Bruise Brothers - Alan Shearer and Neil Ruddock (They had a penchant for bruising opponents)
Budgie - John Burridge (Some sort of rhyming slang one suspects)
CMFG or *Chris Marsden Football Genius* – Chris Marsden (After a wonder goal against Ipswich)
Jesus - Alexander Ostlund (Due to his straggly hair and beard)
One Size - Fitzroy Hall (One size fits all. Get it?)
Chicken George - George Lawrence (After a character in the TV series Roots)
Pedro - Peter Rodriguez (Due to his drooping moustache)

O
Occupations

In these days of players signing for clubs as ten-year-olds and progressing through the system, there are fewer players being signed from non-league football. To have earned a living in the real world is even more of a rarity. Here we bring you a few men who knew what is what was like to get their hands dirty before they entered the fantasy world of full time football.

Jo Tessem (Policeman)
Jo made a late entry into the professional ranks in his native Norway, joining Lyn Oslo at the age of 24. Prior to that he had been a Policeman, his career move proving the theory that a change is as good as ARREST.

Maik Taylor (Soldier)
Maik came from an Army family growing up in and

around North Hampshire. A boyhood Saints fan, he joined the Royal Electrical & Mechanical Engineers regiment and it was whilst representing them and various Hampshire non-league clubs that he came to the attention of Barnet FC. He bought himself out of the services aged 24 to sign professional for them.

Frankie Bennett (Waiter)
Frankie was working as a waiter at a Birmingham hotel whilst playing part-time for Halesowen Town, when Saints signed him in February 1993. He had just turned 24. There is a pattern emerging here.

Jimmy Case (Electrician)
Jimmy was an apprentice electrician and played part-time for South Liverpool when he was signed for their more illustrious neighbours at the tender age of 19.

Keith Cassells (Postman)
Keith didn't deliver much in the way of goals in his short career at The Dell, which was a surprise as delivering was his speciality. He worked as a postman before joining the full time ranks with Watford, aged 20.

Iain Dowie (Rocket Scientist)
Iain was rejected by Saints at the age of 16 and turned to academia, taking a Masters Degree in Engineering at the University of Hertfordshire. He worked with British Aerospace, before joining the professional ranks aged 23, prompting his nickname of Rocket Man. Mind you he seemed to have forgotten just what he had learned at BA in the 2007 court case between himself and Crystal Palace Chairman Simon

Iain Dowie

Jordan, after all it isn't rocket science that if someone's number appears on your phone bill, you can hardly claim to have not spoken to them.

Jon Gittens (Tailor)
Jon had just completed a tailoring qualification when Saints noticed him playing for Paget Rangers. If he was heading for a career in menswear he soon had to "jacket" in and "turn up" for training at The Dell, joining Saints aged 21 in 1985.

Bruce Grobbelaar (Soldier)
Bruce always put his nerves of steel down to the fact that he had served with the Rhodesian National Guard. He saw two years active service during the Rhodesian Bush War, 1975-77. He joined Vancouver Whitecaps before playing for Liverpool and moved to The Dell in 1994.

Barry Horne (Student)
Barry was spotted by Wrexham playing part time for Rhyl, however he didn't sign straight away. He gained a first-class degree in chemistry at Liverpool University before joining the professional ranks at Wrexham, aged 22. Having retired from football, he now works as a chemistry teacher at a school in Chester.

Terry Paine (Railway coach-builder)
Even the longest-serving player in the club's history

Jimmy Case

didn't start his working life as a footballer. Paine had been working as an apprentice coachbuilder in the Eastleigh railway works for two years before Saints spotted him playing for Winchester City aged 17 and snapped him up. (See also Terry Paine)

Andy Townsend (Computer Operator)
Andy was working for Greenwich Borough Council and spending his days in front of a computer screen, when Saints spotted him playing for Weymouth in 1985, at the age of 22. It kick-started what would become a long career in football.

One Club Men
A handful of players spent their entire career at Saints and didn't play for another league club either at home or abroad. Youngsters who bowed out of league football after only a handful of games are not included in this group, neither are members of the current squad. It's interesting to note that in the main, the One Club Men weren't the obvious suspects.

Ted Bates
Pedants might like to point out that Ted was actually signed from Norwich City, but the fact is, after signing on his 19th birthday, he was a Saint for ever more. (See also Ted Bates)

Stan Clements
Stan was just about to turn 24 when he made his league debut for Saints in 1947. He played 120 games for the club scoring one goal before departing for Basingstoke in 1954/55 season.

Eric Day
Another whose entry into football was delayed by the fact that Hitler had got upset with Pompey winning the FA Cup and declared war. Eric was 25 before he made his debut in 1946, but he still played well past his 35th birthday totting up 422 games and 158 goals in the process. (See also Eric Day)

Bill Ellerington
Southampton born, although he was brought up in Sunderland, Bill joined Saints after the war and vied with Alf Ramsey for the right back spot. After Ramsey left for Tottenham Hotspur, Ellerington stayed and clocked up 237 games scoring 11 times in ten seasons. After retiring he was employed as coach, reserve team coach and then chief scout until his retirement in 1980. Bill is credited as being the man who discovered Mick Channon.

Nick Holmes
Southampton born and bred, his career spanned 13 years and throughout that time there was never any doubt that there would only be one club for Nick. (See Nick Holmes)

Matthew Le Tissier
It's fitting that the man known as Le God never wore a shirt for another club side, although he came mighty close to joining Spurs at one point. (See Matthew Le Tissier)

Steve Mills
Ironically Steve was born in Portsmouth, the grandson of Jock Gilfillan, Pompey's goalkeeper in the 1934 FA Cup Final. Steve looked set for a long and distinguished career with Saints after breaking into the side aged just 19. England Under-23 caps followed and all looked rosy before Steve was injured in a car crash in February 1975. His injuries ultimately finished his professional career.

In 1986 Steve discovered he had Leukaemia and dedicated the remaining years of his life to raising funds for research, including a benefit game at The Dell in which a full house saw some great ex-Saints return to help out. Sadly, Steve died a few months later. His 81 appearances have never been forgotten and neither has the illness that killed him, as it remains the charity of choice for Saints supporters.

John Page
He was discovered as a schoolboy and made his league debut at 18. Over the next nine years he made 216 appearances scoring 25 goals in the process, but in 1961 he suffered a slipped disc. That, along with the arrival of Tony Knapp, finished his career at The Dell.

He had the opportunity to stay in the League and join Torquay but opted instead to join Hastings. His league career was over at the age of 27.

Pat Parker
Pat slipped through the net in his native Devon and didn't join the professional ranks till after his 22nd birthday in 1951. It wasn't to be plain sailing for Parker though. He broke a leg in a friendly in his first season and then broke it again in another friendly a year later, but he recovered to become a fixture in the Saints defence. He played 145 games before dropping out of League football, joining Poole and then Cowes.

Tommy Traynor
Tommy enjoyed a 14-year career at The Dell after coming over from Ireland, where he'd played for Dundalk. But any man who plays 487 games after joining as a teenager, has the right to call themselves a one club man .

Len Wilkins
Born in Southampton, Len played for ten years from his debut in 1948 until his retirement aged 32. He racked up 275 games and 3 goals. When he left Saints in April 1958, he had decided to emigrate to Canada and as he took a final wave to the fans at The Dell he received a rousing ten-minute standing ovation.

Len Stansbridge
Len was the goalkeeper in the Southampton Schools side that won the English Schools trophy in 1932. He made his debut in 1938, aged 20. After war was declared he joined the Royal Army Medical Corps and stayed behind with the wounded at Dunkirk. He spent the next five years a prisoner of war. He returned in 1945 and spent the next eight years as reserve team keeper, stepping in whenever the need arose. He never made the position his own, making only 52 appearances in a career that spanned 15 years.

Len gave up his goalkeeping gloves for gardening ones and joined the council as a groundsman at the Sports Centre before becoming groundsman at The Dell in 1962. He was a familiar sight riding his bike from his Shirley home to The Dell every day. He held the position until 1984 when he retired aged 65. Len might have the least number of appearances of our One Club Men, but he almost certainly spent more time on The Dell pitch than any other Saints player. Sadly Len died only two years after retiring.

Oldest Player
The oldest player to turn out for Saints is Bruce Grobbelaar, who was 38 years, 6 months and 2 days old, when he made his final appearance for the club in a 0-3 defeat at Villa Park in 1996.

One Game Wonders
The following players made only one appearance for the club post war.

Derek Allan	v. Man City (h) 1 May 1993 (sub)
Antonio Almeida	v. Arsenal (h) 18 Sept 1999 (sub)
Ryan Ashford	v. Mansfield Town (a) 26 Sept 2000
Colin Cramb	v. Everton (a) 4 Dec 1993 (sub)
Sandie Davie	v. Man Utd (a) 20 Feb 1971
Richard Davis	v. Plymouth Argyle (a) 17 Feb 1954
Kevin Dawtry	v. Nottingham F (a) 2 May 1979 (sub)
Ali Dia	v. Leeds Utd (h) 23 Nov 1996 (sub)
Jose Callego	v. Barnsley (a) 2 October 1948
Mervyn Gill	v. Walsall (a) 28 Apr 1956
Tony Heaney	v. Brighton (h) 17 Sept 1960
Colin Holmes	v. Wrexham (a) 9 April 1960
Martin McGrath	v. Leeds Utd (a) 8 March 1980
Bill Molloy	v. Blackburn Rovers (h) 22 Oct 1949
Paul Murray	v. Tottenham (A) 9 Sept 2001(sub)
Bernard Pask	v. Coventry (a) Mar 28 1960
Wayne Pratt	v. Leeds Utd (h) 22 Nov 1980
Alastair Spedding	v. Rotherham Utd (a) 8 Nov 1983
Peter Vine	v. Bury (a) 21 Mar 1959
Peter Whiston	v. Newcastle Utd (a) 27 Aug 1994

(Correct to end of 2006/07)

Peter Osgood (FA Cup Hero)
Whilst Ossie had his best days in a Chelsea shirt, Saints best days were when Peter wore one of ours.

Saints never overtook Chelsea in Peter's affections, but by his own admission, they came close. Right up to his death on March 1st 2006, he lived in the Southampton area alternating between watching Chelsea and Saints.

SOUTHAMPT... FOOTBALL

Peter Osgood on the day he signed for Saints in 1974

fell out of love with the game.

Incensed by the antics of Blackburn trouble maker John Bailey, that had seen him get Steve Williams sent off, Ossie dispatched Bailey with a head butt. He walked off the field in a Saints shirt for the last time. Bailey was never forgotten by Saints fans and he could not play a game against them without being booed for 90 minutes right up to the end of his career.

Osgood returned to Chelsea after a period in the States. He worked in hospitality at Stamford Bridge and wrote his autobiography *Ossie - King of Stamford Bridge.*

When he arrived in March 1974 he was a club record signing at £275,000. He was manager McMenemy's gamble to avoid relegation

Sadly after months in dispute at Stamford Bridge, Ossie wasn't fit enough to make a difference. Two years later he was influential, playing a full part in the FA Cup win.

Perhaps his champagne moment for Saints was in the quarter final at Bradford City. In a tense match it needed that touch of genius and four minutes before the break it came. Saints got a free kick 25-yards out. Ossie flipped the ball up and Jim McCalliog volleyed it past a startled keeper for the game's only goal.

The night of the FA Cup triumph, so the story goes, Ossie took the cup home with him. "I've slept with worse," was his response.

Ossie remained loyal to Saints and enjoyed a swansong in the European Cup Winners Cup. In Saints promotion year, 1977-78, he started the season in fine form, missing only one game and scoring three times, but at Blackburn on a cold Guy Fawkes night, Ossie finally

He was fondly remembered and loved in Southampton right up until his premature death, aged 59.

Tributes poured in, including this one from Mick Channon. "He was a great character and a fantastic player. He was out on his own for a few years. Probably the only one who could touch him was George Best - he was that good."

Sadly Ossie and Saints legend Charlie Wayman died in the same week. Southampton paid tribute to them both with a round of applause before the home match against Coventry City on March 4th, 2006. The players worn black armbands.
1974-78. 161 Apps. 36 Goals.

Own Goals

Perhaps the weirdest own goal ever scored by a Saints player was at Derby County in November 2001. The Rams had a corner and they tried to lay it to the edge of the box. James Beattie took a big swing at the ball but instead of clearing it, he sent it soaring into orbit before it dropped directly over the goal.

Keeper Paul Jones at first left the ball, then went to cover, it before finally deciding that it might just go in after all. By then it was too late and it dropped into the goal just under the bar.

Jones later complained that the ball had gone out and come back in with the wind. Unfortunately it was the only goal of the game and left Gordon Strachan saying that he "will never see another goal like it in football."

Old Foes

The following are defunct or former league clubs who Southampton have played league games against since joining the league in 1920.

Aberdare
Accrington Stanley
Aldershot
Bradford Park Avenue
Exeter City
Gateshead
Merthyr Town
Nelson
Newport County
Oxford United
South Shields
Torquay United
York City

P

Terry Paine

Without a doubt Terry Paine is one of only three players who can truly claim to be the greatest ever to pull on a Saints shirt. (The others being Mick Channon and Matthew Le Tissier.) But if you talk to a Saints fan over the age of 60, then there is only one candidate for the title greatest player and that's Terry Lionel Paine, MBE.

Playing for Winchester City as a 17-year-old, Paine attracted the attentions of both Pompey and Arsenal before Southampton manager Ted Bates

nipped in quickly and got his man. Paine gave up his job at Eastleigh rail works and made his reserve team debut, a week later. He was seven days short of his 18th birthday. In March 1957 he made his first team debut at home to Brentford. He ended the season with 9 appearances and 2 goals to his name and was barely to miss a game for the next 17 years.

He starred in Saints rise from the Third Division to the top flight and won the first of 19 England caps in May 1963. He played against Mexico in the 1966 World Cup Finals, although he wouldn't make the Final itself. Sadly that was to be his last England game as Alf Ramsey developed his wingless wonders strategy.

The 27-year-old Paine had the consolation of First Division football for the first time, the following season and the arrival of Ron Davies triggered Paine's greatest period with the club. Time and time again got to the goal line and put a pinpoint cross onto Davies' head.

The demise of wingers coincided with Terry reaching his thirties. He adapted and dropped back into midfield. His pin-point passing was a major reason why Mick Channon pushed himself into the England reckoning. Even at this stage, he barely missed a game. When he did, it wasn't through any lack of fitness. It tended to be his penchant to commit the odd niggly foul and tot up the disciplinary points.

The arrival of Lawrie McMenemy was to signal the end of his Saints career. His last game for the club was at Burnley in the penultimate game of the relegation season, 1973-74. In fact the final game was the only one he would miss all season.

Many fans believed that if Paine was still good enough in the top flight even at 35 he would be a revelation in

Terry Paine in action in 1972

the Second Division. Sadly he was not to play for the club again.

McMenemy, not the most popular man in the City at that point, perhaps saw Paine as a threat. Indeed there were those who would have liked to have seen Terry given the manager's job after relegation. He was released to join Hereford United as player-coach. He would grace the Dell pitch twice more though, firstly in his testimonial against Ipswich Town in April 1975. Then, in an emotional moment in October 1976, a guard of honour led by Mick Channon, clapped him onto the pitch with his Hereford side. He would end the season by setting the League record for appearances, finishing on 819 games.

After retiring as a player, he took up various coaching positions and after spending a lot of time in South Africa during the 1990s, emigrated there for good. He lives there to this day, earning a living as the country's most respected football pundit.
1957-76. 811 (4) Apps. 187 Goals.

David Peach (FA Cup Hero)

David Peach was Lawrie McMenemy's first signing, arriving from Gillingham in January 1974. He was converted to an attacking left back, and was an ever-present during the 1976 FA Cup run. He missed only one game in all competitions that season.

After both Mick Channon and Jim McCalliog had missed penalties earlier in the season, Peach became the designated penalty taker. By the time of the FA Cup semi-final he hadn't yet taken a spot kick for the club. 1-0 up against Crystal Palace, Southampton were given a penalty. Peach stepped up knowing that with only ten minutes left, Saints were surely at Wembley, but if he missed, it might hand the impetus back to Palace.

If he was nervous, it didn't show and he coolly dinked the ball into the middle of the goal, correctly guessing that keeper Hammond would dive one way or the other.

Peach was one of only two survivors for the return trip to Wembley in 1979, for the League Cup Final. Both he and the other man, Nick Holmes, scored that day, showing that it wasn't just penalties he could net from. Indeed in August 1979 he became the highest scoring full back in the league.

His Saints career was longer than most of his cup final colleagues. In fact he was unlucky not to get a full England cap when he went on a tour of South America with the full squad in 1977.

It was a surprise when he was sold to lower league Swindon Town for £150,000, still aged only 29, in 1980.

David Peach

After retiring from football he remained in the area, living in the New Forest and running a building business. He coaches local football sides to this day. 1974-80. 278 (4) Apps. 44 Goals.

Penalty Shoot Outs

Southampton's first experience of settling a match with a penalty shoot out came in the 1985/86 season. After two scoreless draws with Millwall in the two-legged League Cup second round, they won through on penalties.

Perhaps their greatest triumph came in the FA Cup fourth round replay against Manchester United in 1992. After a 0-0 draw at The Dell, few gave Saints much hope at Old Trafford.

A Sky TV audience were shocked to see the visitors go 2-0 up in 22 minutes through Stuart Gray and Alan Shearer. United pulled one back on the stroke of half time but as the game reached the 90th minute it looked like Saints would hold out and record their first FA Cup win against United at any ground (apart from Wembley).

But then United got a fluky last gasp equaliser, when a shot going nowhere hit Jeff Kenna and deflected into the path of Brian McClair who made no mistake. Saints didn't have time to kick off.

Extra time was goalless, so it came down to penalties in front of the Stretford End. This being the first season since the abolition of second replays, it was also the first shoot out between two top flight English sides. Matthew Le Tissier, who had never missed a penalty opted to go last, not because he wanted a psychological advantage or such like, but because he "fancied the glory of scoring the winning penalty."

He would be denied that honour due to the accuracy of his team mates and the brilliance of Tim Flowers. Firstly Neil Ruddock scored for Saints and then Neil Webb missed for United. Sharpe and Irwin both scored for the home side as did Micky Adams, Barry Horne and Alan Shearer for the visitors. With the score at 4-2, up stepped rookie Ryan Giggs needing to score to keep United in the game. He hit it to Flowers' left, and the keeper went the right way, to kept it out. He sprang to his feet and almost qualified for the summer Olympics with a 100 metre dash to the celebrating Saints fans. His team-mates couldn't get near him.

Penalty shoot outs can bring of course bring despair as well as joy. The lowest low for Southampton surely came in 2006/07, in the Championship play-off semi final at Pride Park. Derby County remained calm whilst Inigo Idiakez and then Leon Best, blazed wide. A return to the Premier League was not going to happen for Saints this time.

Pitch Invasions

As Saints played their last home game before the FA Cup Final in 1976, the final whistle was greeted with a good natured pitch invasion. The supporters congratulated their heroes and then demanded that they take the applause of the crowd from the directors box.

This started a tradition that was to continue for many years after the last home game of the season, as the players would run for their lives while fans tried to get a souvenir from the day. The players would usually throw their kit to the crowd. It was never violent and the Police always saw to it that the visiting supporters weren't intimidated or indeed, joined in.

However in the 1980s, the club started to become increasingly concerned about the tradition. More and more fans were getting onto the pitch. Many would also get into the stand surrounding the directors box. It was a miracle that no one had been injured either by falling out of the stand or in the mêlée as supporters clamoured to catch a shirt.

In 1989, new terrace hero Neil Ruddock left the field after the game against Manchester United completely naked after being engulfed by supporters who stripped him of everything. In fairness, the player himself didn't appear too bothered about it and, even seemed to relish the chance to streak back to the dressing room without being arrested.

The end of the tradition came in 1992. Saints escaped off the field after beating Oldham Athletic and reappeared in the stand to take the applause.

The pitch was being re-laid in the summer and some supporters decided to dig up a bit of it to take home. A few turfs were aimed good naturedly towards the players in the directors box, who made the mistake of joining in the fun by lobbing them back. Whether this was the day that the phrase "turf war" was coined is unsure, but soon large clumps of The Dell pitch were flying backwards and forwards through the air.

The local paper insinuated that this was something more sinister than end of season high jinks – that the fans were having a go at the players for what had been the worst season in two decades – but they couldn't have been more wrong. It was all just good clean fun.

Whatever the reason though, the club along with the Police decided that this tradition could continue no longer.

The following season, in 1992, strong warnings were issued to the fans.

Augmented by a ring of stewards at the final whistle of the last home game, it was also announced that instead of throwing their shirts to the crowd, the team would do a lap of honour. The Daily Echo would publish pictures of randomly selected fans. Those pictured would win a shirt worn in the game. It was added that if anyone did encroach onto the pitch, then the players would not come out and no shirts would be given away in the paper.

It worked and the traditional end of season pitch invasion had gone for ever. Or had it? After Matthew Le Tissier had secured a fairytale ending for The Dell in the final League game against Arsenal, the fans couldn't be kept back and poured on to the pitch at the final whistle. They returned to the terraces when requested, so the players could come out to take a final bow.

Plastic Pitches

Saints played their first game on plastic when they travelled to Queens Park Rangers in the 1983/84 season. It could be said that Saints were in their greatest-ever period of football having just reached the FA Cup semi final and were in the middle of a run that would see them finish runners-up in the league. However all those games had been played on grass and Saints couldn't quite get the hang of this new-fangled plastic.

With just over an hour gone, they found themselves 0-4 down. The following season they travelled to Loftus Road in the Milk Cup for a replay and acquitted themselves well even missing a late penalty to leave the game scoreless at the end of extra time. In the second replay, again on plastic, Saints took another 4-0 hammering.

Revenge and indeed the club's first win on an artificial surface, came later in the 1984-85 season in the League. Saints hit four with no reply, thus winning and scoring at the fourth attempt. Joe Jordan went into the record books as the first man to score for Saints on plastic.

Southampton would play another three games on QPR's plastic surface, winning one and losing two, to give an overall record of played 7, won 2, lost 4. In 1988 the Loftus Road club – the first to lay an Astroturf pitch – became the first club to tear one up.

If Saints thought that QPR's pitch didn't suit them, then they had yet to encounter Luton Town's version at Kenilworth Road. The Hatters took a little longer to get on the plastic bandwagon, not laying theirs till 1985.

Saints, by now, might have been expected to have adjusted to plastic. Er, no.

The team looked like they were on an illegal version of grass rather than an imitation one and were hammered 7-0. Ironically QPR were visiting The Dell the following week and were thumped 3-0, to score a victory for good old mud & grass.

Sadly there would be two more seven-goal thrillers at Kenilworth Road. Saints did at least manage to win one of them in 1988/89. Even in the one win when they still took it to the wire, conceding three.

Saints record on Luton's surface was so bad, the team almost looked forward to a trip to QPR. In eight games at Kenilworth Road, they won only once, drew 3 and lost 4. In typical Saints fashion, the sole victory was in their last visit before the pitch was torn up.

Saints only got to play on Oldham Athletic's Astroturf/sand blend on one occasion, a Littlewoods cup replay. The home side showed they knew how to play on it and sent Saints skidding to a 0-2 defeat.

The League finally banned Astroturf pitches and decreed that they all be torn up at the end of the 1990/91 season. A collective sigh of relief could be heard all over the country, but probably more at The Dell than anywhere else.

There was one other English club who laid an Astroturf surface and that was Preston North End. Luckily for Southampton, the two teams' paths did not cross during this time. A look at Saints record on plastic is enough to bring any St Mary's regular out in a cold sweat. It reads :
Played 16. Won 3. Drawn 4. Lost 9
Goals for 18. Goals against 37

Player-Managers

Although a total of five former players have managed Southampton, strangely the club has have never had a player-manager.

Player Of The Year

Strangely, Southampton didn't have a player of the year award until 1974, when the club, in conjunction with local paper, The Daily Echo, introduced the award, voted for by the supporters. It has been won by 34 players, the positional breakdown is:

Goalkeepers 7
Defenders   10
Midfielders 6
Forwards   8
Le Tissier   3

1974. Mike Channon
1975. Mel Blyth
1976. David Peach
1977. Steve Williams
1978. Alan Ball
1979. Malcolm Waldron

Glenn Cockerill

1980. Phil Boyer
1981. Ivan Golac
1982. Kevin Keegan
1983. Mark Wright
1984. David Armstrong
1985. Peter Shilton
1986. Peter Shilton
1987. Glenn Cockerill
1988. Derek Statham

1989. Jimmy Case
1990. Matt LeTissier
1991. Alan Shearer
1992. Tim Flowers
1993. Tim Flowers
1994. Matt LeTissier
1995. Matt LeTissier
1996. Dave Beasant
1997. Egil Ostenstad
1998. Paul Jones
1999. James Beattie
2000. Dean Richards
2001. Wayne Bridge
2002. Chris Marsden
2003 James Beattie
2004 Antti Niemi
2005 Peter Crouch
2006 Claus Lundekvam
2007 Chris Baird

Ten "Saints Greats" never to win the award (175 games plus since inauguration).
1. Nick Holmes
2. Danny Wallace
3. Steve Moran
4. Chris Nicholl
5. Ken Monkou
6. Jason Dodd
7. Francis Benali
8. Neil Maddison
9. Matt Oakley
10. Kevin Moore

Pre-Match Entertainment

Back in the good old days at The Dell, the crowd were entertained pre-match, by The Albion Band. A local brass band, they would play various instrumental pieces. As the 1960s came to an end and the nation started to tune in to "pop" music, the Albion Band were replaced by a DJ.

Catering for the younger supporters, he was often augmented by one-off visits from the likes of the RAF Police dog Display Team (see Dogs). In April 1975, there was even as an athletics meeting.

The mid-1970s saw other local bands occasionally play on the hallowed turf, including the Excelsior New Orleans Jazz band and perennial crowd favourites The Romsey Old Boys Cadet Band, who each year would appear in a different fancy dress costume. Unforgettable was the sight of 30 Woodpeckers marching in line across the pitch playing the Woody Woodpecker theme.

The 1990s saw the arrival of Sky TV and to herald the new era of televised football, they supplied the pre-match entertainment. It included the Sky Strikers, an array of scantily clad dancers and a few miming pop stars of the day. So it was that we had the pleasure of the company of Curiosity Killed The Cat.

The Valley Slags performance (see Valley Slags) went down in footballing history, as did resident DJ Howard Bowden's spinning of Freddie Mercury's song Barcelona. It wasn't that the massed hordes of the home counties Manchester United fans and Sir Alex and had anything against the moustachioed Queen singer, but as they had just been beaten by the Spanish giants, it rubbed a raw nerve. This led to Bowden's departure from the booth, an FA warning to the Club and the headline "Barceloony" in the Daily Star.

The move to St Mary's saw many supporters favourite ever pre match entertainment. In the inaugural game in the new stadium against Espanyol, opening ceremonies were interrupted by a topless young lady attempting to, lets say, get abreast of the situation. This stirred up a few more ladies in the crowd to join in and the game itself was interrupted on more than one occasion.

2006 brought local comedian Mike Osman and his Matchday Mayhem. The Lowlight arguably was when

The Bedford

Eastenders actor John Bardon (Jim Brennan in the soap) conducted the crowd. It could only get better after that.

Pubs
The Bedford
Due to its vicinity to The Dell, the Bedford was for many years considered THE pub for Saints supporters. In the 1940/50s it was the headquarters of the Supporters Club and it enjoyed a resurgence of popularity in the final decade or so of the old ground's existence.

The Fitzhugh
Not quite the closest pub to The Dell, being situated in Milton Road, it was nevertheless the pub of choice for home supporters for many years. In 1980 it changed its name to the Corner Post along with a new sign showing Kevin Keegan taking a corner and it kept this name to the mid-1990s, when it once again reverted to its original moniker. In the last years of The Dell, crowds would spill out onto the street, as it was the final watering hole before the ground.

The Warren's
Despite being in the centre of town, a good mile from The Dell, it was popular amongst a certain section of the support from 1975 until its closure in 1980. However, it got a bad reputation after a riot involving Millwall supporters in 1979. They were in the city for a cup tie with Salisbury being played at The Dell. The writing was on the wall and in September 1980 it shut its doors reopening as a late night wine bar called Boogie's.

The Lord Louis
In the shadow of the Civic Centre Clock, this pub had always been a focal point for Saints fans and with the closure of the Warrens it enjoyed a surge in popularity from 1980-83. The Louis was finally closed it in 1987 to make way for the Marland's shopping centre.

The Painted Wagon
In 1983 this became the adopted home of the Southampton "Casuals" and for a couple of years was a real Saints stronghold, before closing to become a Mongolian themed restaurant. Lately it has reopened again as a bar.

The Winston
The nearest pub to The Dell, it did most of its trade with visiting supporters, being at the Away end of the ground in Archers Road. It's still open today despite the loss of trade when Saints moved home.

The Gateway Hotel
Tucked away in Northlands Road it was a little gem for Saints supporters and aided by a home fans-only policy. For those who knew to go around to the back door, it became very popular in the mid 1980s right up until the closure of The Dell. Half way between both the County ground and The Dell, it must have seen a big drop in trade when both football and cricket clubs moved in the same year, 2001.

The Grapes
With the move to St Mary's the Grapes in Oxford Street became popular with Saints supporters between 2001-2005. However, as it got busier, the prices went through the roof and many Saints fans headed for other hostelries.

The Angelsea
With its proximity to the new stadium, the Angelsea Tavern attracted a football clientele on match days. It soon attracted a new owner who re-christened it The Le Tissier's Feet and festooned the bar with Saints related memorabilia. However, trade on non-match days was less than brisk, due to the location and the pub was again sold. It underwent another name change, this time to The Chapel after the area its located in.

The Zeb Bar
Situated in St Mary's Street, this pub was known for many years as The Oddfellows. Located in the shadow of St Mary's Church, it is likely that some of the men who formed the club may have quenched their thirst in the bar. In 2006 it came into new ownership and got a stripey new look and a new name, the Zeb Bar. The latest edition to the list of essential Saints watering holes.

Q
The Queen
If anyone wonders which football team HM The Queen supports, Saints fans will refer them back to the last domestic game she attended, namely the 1976 FA Cup Final.

The evidence does not stop there. She wore a blue outfit on the day, signifying her support for the team in yellow & blue, and the beaming smile she displayed as she handed the cup over should leave no one in any doubt as to who she wanted to win.

It's rumoured that afterwards she vowed never to watch another final at Wembley unless Saints were participating, and she has kept to her word. Despite being Queen of Wales as well, she couldn't bring herself to cross the River Severn in 2003. Now that the final has returned to Wembley it's believed that each year the Queen keeps Cup Final weekend free in case her beloved Saints once again reach the final. She still has hopes that she can hand the cup over for a return to the city, which if she had her way, would surely be the capital.

NB. The publishers would like to point out that some of this information might not be strictly accurate but that's the official secrets act for you.

Quickest Ever Goal
Many Saints fans believe that Matt Le Tissier's 28-second goal against Liverpool on Valentines Day 1994 was the fastest ever goal by a Southampton player. Although it's certainly the fastest televised goal, there have been quicker.

Some would say that Graham Baker's effort against Blackpool in November 1977 was quicker but they would be wrong, although certain sources claim it is the fastest goal by a Saints debutant. They are all wrong though. The winner is Tommy Mulgrew, who on the opening day of 1954/55 season, making is debut after signing from Newcastle United, scored after only 15 seconds.

The fastest goal by a visiting player is Coventry City's Mark Hateley, who scored after only 14 seconds, in the one-all draw in January 1983.

Quotes
"Kenny Dalglish has about as much personality as a tennis racket." *Mike Channon.*

"The opening ceremony was good, although I missed it." *Graeme Le Saux.*

"I'd like to play for an Italian club like Barcelona." *Mark Draper.*

"The minute's silence was immaculate, I have never heard a minute's silence like that." *Glenn Hoddle.*

"One accusation you can't throw at me is that I've always done my best." *Alan Shearer*

"I don't think there is anybody bigger or smaller than Maradona." *Kevin Keegan.*

"The important thing is he shook hands with us over the phone." *Alan Ball.*

"Football's all about 90 minutes." *Glenn Hoddle*

"When a player gets to 30, so does his body." *Glenn Hoddle.*

"Okay, so we lost, but good things can come from it - negative and positive." *Glenn Hoddle.*

"You only get one opportunity of an England debut." *Alan Shearer.*

"He's started anticipating what's going to happen before it's even happened." *Graeme Le Saux.*

"The referee has a reputation for trying to make a name for himself." *Graeme Souness.*

"When you are 4-0 up you should never lose 7-1." *Lawrie McMenemy.*

"When Neil (Lennon) played for me, he ran his legs off." *Lawrie McMenemy.*

"The last player to score a hat-trick in a FA Cup final was Stan Mortensen. He even had a final named after him - the Matthews Final." *Lawrie McMenemy.*

"Overall I think we dominated for 75% of the game, but we have to make sure we do that for the other 15." *Dave Jones*

"I don't read everything I read in the press." *Dave Jones*

"Although we are playing Russian Roulette we are obviously playing Catch 22 at the moment and it's a difficult scenario to get my head round." *Paul Sturrock*

R

Sir Alf Ramsey

Many of the London-based so-called football experts would have you believe that England's World Cup victory was all down to the footballing academy of West Ham United, but they would be wrong. The master tactician who managed the side started his professional football career and learnt his trade at The Dell.

The problem was that Saints had the two finest right backs in the country in Ramsey and Bill Ellerington and they vied for the number two shirt not just at Saints but with England as well. After Ramsey returned from injury in the latter part of the 1948/49 season, he found Ellerington in command of both shirts and decided his future lay elsewhere. A move to Tottenham Hotspur followed.

In the close season of 1954 it was strongly rumoured that Sir Alf, or plain Alf as he was then, might be returning as player-coach. This was prior to the appointment of Ted Bates. It might have changed the history of the club completely, but Ramsey stayed at Spurs another year before he joined Ipswich Town where honed his managerial skills. There can be no doubt, though, as to where he set his footballing standards and to which club the grateful nation should owe a great debt.
1944-49. 96 Apps. 8 Goals.

Records

In 1973, Southampton's first team squad followed other prominent teams and released a record,

Sir Alf Ramsey in 1949 and (below) The Saints Song

entitled "The Saints Song." It was released on the Phillips label with a catalogue number of 6006.312.1. Written by Duncan Campbell, it was a jaunty little song, pretty much bog standard for the time.

The B side simply called "The Saints" was merely the squad introducing themselves set to music, with the small change that goalkeeper Eric Martin announces himself as a forward followed by a Wiltshire burr stating, "I'm Mick Channon and I play in Goal."

Chorus
We are Southampton, we play down at the Dell
We're better known to most as just the Saints
We might not be one of the bigger clubs unlike some of the rest
But one day you'll see we will become the best

Verses
1. We haven't been up in the first division long
And we're learning more with every game we play
We've yet to win the FA Cup or win the league
But we know we're going to get them both some day

2. Red & Whites the colours that we're proud to wear
Especially when we hear the crowd all yell
We mustn't let the Northern boys or London lads
Take all the glory we want some as well.

It's a Record!

'The Saints Song' on sale in the
Saints Souvenir Shop, Price 45p

*3.And now we've made a record we would like to
say
A special thanks to all our many fans
Who support us when we play at home on
Saturday's
On the terraces and up in the stands*

It will be no surprise to anyone to learn that it didn't
trouble the charts. However, when Saints reached the
FA Cup Final in 2003, the catchy "Southampton Boys"
by The Red & White Machines was released. The B
side was the sublime, Brazilian-influenced,
"Marsdeniho."

The band fronted by MC Alistair and Power FM's

Peter Hood took their CD to number 16 in the National
Charts .

Derek Reeves

Derek Reeves joined Saints after completing his
National Service in 1954. After a season in the
reserves, he made his debut in the final games of the
1954/55 season, scoring against his home town club
Bournemouth. This was just a taste of things to come.
Derek wouldn't be top scorer in his first full season, but
he would top the club's goalscoring charts for the next
four years.

In Saints promotion year of 1959/60, Derek scored no
less than 39 goals from 46 games. It remains a Division
Three record.

The following season, he found goals harder to come by, scoring only ten in the league although in the League cup he was prolific, scoring eight. This included all five in a fourth round tie against Leeds United. In seven years at The Dell, Derek scored goals at a phenomenal rate and is the seventh highest scorer in Southampton's history.

His final game would be against Scunthorpe United in 1962 and he was sold to Bournemouth for £8,000, still aged only 28. In later years he was an ambulance driver, sadly dying in May 1995. 1955-62. 311 Apps. 173 Goals.

George Reader (right)

Referee

How many football clubs can claim that one of their players became a World Cup Final referee and chairman of the club for good measure? Southampton can.

George Reader first arrived at the Dell as player in 1920, but after only three appearances he moved to non-league Cowes on the Isle of Wight. By then he had taken up a post as a schoolmaster in Southampton and after finishing playing, refereed his first match on The Common. Within six years he was running the line for League matches and in 1939 he refereed his first League match. After his third game, the League was suspended as war broke out.

Reader refereed many wartime games including cup finals, but by the time hostilities had ceased, he was too old to referee in the Football League. However, in Europe they had no such worries and he was much in demand, refereeing many internationals. So much so, that in 1948 the Football League took the unprecedented step of asking him to come out of domestic retirement.

In 1950 he accompanied the England team to the World cup in Brazil and officiated in the opening game between the hosts and Mexico, and a group game between Uruguay and Bolivia. His bearing impressed everyone, to the extent that he was appointed to referee the final between Brazil and Uruguay.

Estimates of the attendance in the Maracana stadium that day vary between 174,000 up to 250,000, both of which would have been more than lived in Southampton at the time. Even the lower figure is the largest recorded attendance at any football match ever. Brazil lost, but neither side had anything but praise for the referee.

Reader returned home to Hanley Road – a mere drop kick from The Dell. He retired from refereeing, continuing to teach. George accepted an invitation to join the Southampton board. In 1963 he was made chairman, a position he occupied until his death in 1978 aged 82. Two years earlier he had sat beside the Queen at the FA Cup Final and was perhaps the calmest Saints official in the ground. Well, he had seen it all before.

Relegation

Southampton Football Club have only been relegated on three occasions. Their first taste of that sickening feeling came in 1952/53 when they were relegated from the Second Division to the old Third Division (S). They had graced the competition for 31 years. The drop came after two comfortable mid-table finishes and indeed only three years after losing out on promotion by goal average.

Many excuses were given, including injury and bad luck, but the team had been in the bottom two since November, apart from a brief two week spell. Despite only one defeat in the last eight games, it was too late to save them.

Southampton would not suffer the same fate until the 1973/74 season, when after eight seasons in the top flight, they found themselves the first victims of the new three up, three down rule. The popular myth is that Manchester United were the first to suffer, but United finished four points adrift of Saints and would have still gone down under the previous season's rules.

In truth it had been a nightmare season for Saints. Right up to the turn of the year they seemed to be going well under new manager Lawrie McMenemy and lay in 8th spot. But then they started to plummet. They would win only three games out of the final 19, including a 3-0 win at Everton on the final day, that was too little, too late.

In the end it was tight, with only one point in it. Indeed five clubs were within two points of them. In fact the club didn't actually drop into the relegation zone until the penultimate game of the season, but they found to their cost the only placing that matters is the final one.

The third and hopefully, final, occasion Saints went down was in 2004/05. A squad that been in the FA Cup Final only two years previously and had enjoyed a run of five comfortable mid-table finishes, suddenly paid the price of the club employing four managers in the calendar year of 2004.

Harry Redknapp had, quite reasonably, been expected to keep the team up, but he appeared unable to decide on his best team. The collection of highly paid loan signings showed as much fight as Mother Theresa and went down with barely a whimper, while those players with the club at heart, were seemingly ignored and had to watch from the sidelines.

Rock N' Roll

St Mary's Stadium has hosted two big rock and roll concerts to date. The first in the summer of 2005, featured ex-Watford Chairman Elton John, who wowed an all-seated audience. The second concert in June 2006 saw perhaps the biggest attendance at an event at the stadium. The increased capacity of 35,000 – due to standing on the pitch – saw Bon Jovi supported by Nickelback.

The Dell never attempted to stage any similar events during its history, although it's a little-known fact that in the late 1970s, negotiations to host a gig by Rod Stewart got to an advanced stage before eventually falling through.

Peter Rodrigues (FA Cup Hero)

When 31-year-old Peter Rodrigues was given a free transfer by Sheffield Wednesday in the summer of 1975, he could be forgiven for thinking that his career was on the downward slope. But little did he know that the greatest season of his footballing career lay ahead. Initially it was thought that he would be covering for Steve Mills while he recovered from injuries received in a car crash. It became clear, though, that Mills wouldn't start training until April. Rodrigues made the right back spot his own, missing only one game all season, in all competitions.

Peter Rodrigues

Looking back it seems that every player had a champagne moment in the FA Cup run. Peter perhaps didn't, well, not at least until he picked up the cup from the Queen, but he brought a calming influence to the side and was the perfect captain.

The following season Peter was still a regular in the side, but he suffered knee problems and he retired at the end of the season. Initially he became mine host at the King Rufus pub in Eling, working on and off in the licensed trade until moving to Spain in 2002.

However he soon returned to Southampton to live. In 2004 he was dismayed to find that his daughter was selling his FA Cup winners medal. Rupert Lowe stepped in to buy it on behalf of the club and presented it to Peter who promptly donated it back to be displayed in St Mary's. 1975-77. 72 Apps. 3 Goals.

Rugby

History tells us that it was a close call back in 1885 and that Southampton FC could easily have been playing Rugby Football had the voting swung a little in the other direction. However, that wasn't to be the last we saw of the game and on 8th November 1947, The Dell hosted a game between a Hampshire & Sussex XV

taking on the touring Australian Rugby Union side. 8,000 spectators turned out to see the visiting Aussies win 14-5.

A good result considering they had been beaten only once in the 17 games played on the tour to that point.

S
Scored on Debut

The following players have all scored on their League debuts for the club since the war.

Bobby Veck	v. Swansea (h) 1946-47
Joe Mallett	v. Plymouth Argyle(a) 1946-47
Bill Wrigglesworth	v. Coventry City (h) 1947/48
Jack Edwards	v. Grimsby Town (h) 1949-50
Jimmy McGowan	v. Cardiff City (h) 1949-50
Ken Wilkins	v. Birmingham City (a) 1950-51
Johnny Walker	v. Luton Town (h) 1953-54
Tom McGarrity	v. Hull City (h) 1952-53
John Flood	v. Blackburn Rovers (h) 1952-53
Tommy Mulgrew	v. Brentford (h) 1954-55
Jimmy Shields	v. Bournemouth&BA (h) 1956-57
Brian Clifton	v. Brighton & HA (h) 1957-58
Gordon Brown	v. Tranmere Rovers (h) 1959-60
George Kirby	v. Chelsea (h) 1962-63
John McGuigan	v. Swansea Town (h) 1963-64
Norman Dean	v. Norwich City (a) 1965-66
Fred Kemp	v. Preston North End (h) 1965-66
David Webb	v. Wolverhampton W (a)1965-66
Mick Channon	v. Bristol City (h) 1965-66
Bobby Stokes	v. Burnley (h) 1968-69
Graham Baker	v. Blackpool (h) 1977-78
Steve Moran	v. Manchester C (h) 1979-80 (s)
Stuart McManus	v. Queens Park Rngrs (a) 1985-86
Colin Clarke	v. Queens Park Rngrs (h) 1986-87
Gordon Hobson	v. Watford (h) 1986-87
Paul Rideout	v. West Ham United (h) 1988-89
Tahar El Khalej	v. Tottenham H (a) 1999-00
Kevin Phillips	v. Leicester City (a) 2003-04
Leandre Griffitt	v.Blackburn Rvrs (h) 2003/04 (s)
Henri Camara	v. Birmingham City (a) 2005/06(s)
Bradley Wright Phillips	v. Derby County (a) 2006-07 (s)

Sendings Off

The first Saints player to be sent off was Jack Angus, who received his marching orders on February 24th 1894, playing in a Hampshire Senior Cup replay at the County Ground against old enemies Freemantle. Luckily for Angus it didn't stop Saints winning 2-1, although they were to lose the Final 0-1, against the Royal Engineers.

In those days sendings off were rarer than Queen Victoria being amused, not least because hacking was an acceptable form of tackling. Leading amateur side and early cup winners Corinthians refused to accept that a player would deliberately foul another. As Gentlemen they would kick the penalty wide of goal if they were awarded one, but as professionalism came into the game fouls became more frequent.

The first recorded League dismissal came in a Southern League defeat at Sheppey United on January 7th 1899. The doer of the dastardly deed was Arthur Chadwick. It didn't cost them too dearly, as Saints still won the title at the end of the season.

When Saints joined the Football League in 1920, it was only a matter of months before the first dismissal. The offender was Jimmy Moore in a home defeat to Grimsby Town on 4th December. Saints lost the game, but it didn't cost them promotion. They finished five points behind Champions Crystal Palace and only one side went up.

When the Premier League was formed in 1992, it didn't take Saints long to open their red card account. In fact it was in only the second game when Micky Adams gained the distinction being the first Saints to be branded a sinner, when he was dismissed on 19th August 1992, in a 1-3 defeat at Queens Park Rangers.

Alan Shearer (centre) in jovial mood with Neil Ruddock (right) and Dean Radford during his Saints days

Alan Shearer

Shearer was spotted playing for Wallsend boys club in his native Newcastle by the club's North East Scout. From the start it was clear that Saints had a gem and although his league debut as a substitute didn't bring him a debut goal, his full debut against Arsenal on April 9, 1988 was the stuff legends are made of, as the seventeen-year-old hit a hat trick in a 4-2 victory. He is still the youngest scorer of top division hat-trick. Shearer made England Under-21 caps with Saints and is top scorer for them, with 13 goals.

Ironically, in light of his goalscoring exploits at first Blackburn Rovers and then Newcastle United, he was not a particularly prolific goalscorer at

Southampton, despite that hat trick. But then he was playing in a team of marksmen and his job was to lead the line, hold up the ball and play in the likes of Le Tissier, Rod Wallace and even in some attacking formations, Paul Rideout.

It was inevitable that he would move on after winning England honours in 1992 and it was for a then British transfer record of £3.6 million, that he joined Blackburn Rovers. Those that knew Alan as a player at The Dell, remember him not as the dour straight faced TV Pundit, but as a mischievous character always in on a joke.

1988-92. 140 (18) Apps. 43 Goals.

Bert Shelley

Locally born in Romsey, Bert Shelley returned from the Great War and soon attracted the attention of Saints. The club were keen to sign young local talent in preparation for joining the newly formed Third Division of the Football League.

Bert played in the final season of the club's Southern League membership and was a stalwart of the early Football League days. He is eighth in the table of all-time League appearances for the club.

After retiring from playing in 1932, Bert was appointed the club's first Nursery manager. In 1935 he was promoted to first team trainer before following then manager George Kay to Liverpool in 1936.

He would spend the next two decades there, laying down the foundation for the famous coaching set up at Anfield.

1920-31. 448 Apps. 9 Goals.

Shirt Sponsors

Sept 1980-May 1983.
Photocopying giants Rank Xerox had the honour of being the first-ever shirt sponsors of Saints.

Steve Moran with the first sponsor on his shirt

August 1983-May 1984.
Air Florida were the next to feature, although in those days most Saints supporters had a better chance of seeing their team at Wembley than flying to Florida.

August 1984-May 1993.
Local company Draper Tools enjoyed a nine-season run on the front of the shirts in which time, with the introduction of third kits, it was seen plastered across the front of no less than 14 different shirts.

August 1993-May 1995.
Another local company, this time Millbrook-based manufacturers of heaters, Dimplex were the lucky recipients. Sadly for them their two-year tenancy coincided with perhaps the worst home design ever.

August 1995-May 1999.
This time it was the turn of Sheffield based Sanderson who had their moniker on not just Saints shirts, but Sheffield Wednesday as well.

August 1999-May 2006.
Salisbury based insurance company Friends Provident first became involved with Saints in 1999 and would soon have their name not just on the shirts, but the door as well, as their name was also incorporated into the new stadium name. The official title is therefore, Ladies and Gentlemen, "The Friends Provident St Mary's Stadium."

May 2005-Present.
Flybe.com took over from Friends Provident as not only shirt sponsors but main sponsors as well although curiously they did not want to incorporate their name into the title of the stadium. A budget airline, they did however, express a desire to

help fans travel away. Sadly their destinations don't include Burnley, Stoke and Barnsley.

Skates & Scummers

One of the most misquoted and argued debates between Saints and Pompey fans is how both sets of supporters came up with their nickname/term of abuse for their counterparts.

It is true to say however that Portsmouth supporters were the first to coin a name for their rivals from just along the coast. In the late 1960s they started to call Southampton "Scum" and Saints supporters "Scummers." At the time Pompey were at a low period and Saints were on a high. It was true to say that despite some Saints fans hurling the term back at them, most didn't really care.

Pompey fans will claim that the term started a lot earlier. It came from a mythical dock strike in Portsmouth when dockers from Southampton broke picket lines and worked the port. This couldn't be further from the truth.

Firstly Pompey, up until the late 1970s was mainly a naval port. As such, the dockers there were employed by the MOD and not only had they no rights to strike, but they would have needed to be security cleared. The Navy just wouldn't let anyone off the street work in their port.

The private port was very small indeed and had no unions. In fact Southampton dockers have often been regarded as the most militant in the country and over the years fought long and hard to secure better working conditions for stevedores ending the Tally system in the port that saw only casual labour employed.

In fact the story has a real twist. Up until the 1970s, the main cross channel ferry traffic went through Southampton, not Portsmouth. However work was hampered by union agreements and strict working arrangements, that in hindsight were restrictive. Portsmouth ferry port had no unions and therefore could clear cargo through without restriction and the Dock workers there had no qualms about working on ships diverted from strike bound Southampton. So much so, that when the Port of Southampton had its last strike in 1984, completely closing it, Pompey accepted the ships and there they stayed, never to return, even after the strike was over.

The real truth of the matter is that Scum was a convenient moniker for Pompey fans to use and it stuck. Meanwhile after years of indifference and resorting to calling Pompey fans Scummers themselves, the fanzine The Ugly Inside ran a competition in 1989 to find a suitable term of abuse for their neighbours from the East end of the M27.

The winning entry coined the phrase "Skates." Now this wasn't very original. Portsmouth natives had long referred to sailors from the Royal Navy by the same term. Apparently it was because of the sexual practices of matelots (we can't go there in this family publication). The winner however, pointed out that although it wasn't very original, it would sure as hell get up the noses of the Pompey fans. After long protests they resigned themselves to their fate and the mention of the word Skate means only one thing in Southampton.

Songs

Everyone assumes that the club song is "Oh When The Saints Go Marching In," but that hasn't always been the case. In fact, the club had been in existence for some four decades before it was written, sometime in the 1920s. Originally a Dixieland jazz tune, it wasn't until Louis Armstrong recorded a version in the 1930s, that the tune was known outside New Orleans.

It must have taken some time to filter over the Atlantic because in October 1950 the Supporters Association decided to adopt "The Bells of St Mary's" as the club's theme tune. This ditty was better known at the time than "Oh When…" having been the title track of the 1945 film of the same name, starring Bing Crosby & Ingrid Bergman.

A local musician Monty Warlock, was commissioned to write some special lyrics.

The bells of St Mary's
A message are bringing
Its play up and win now
As cheers round you roll

So up for Saints and win boys
For victory we're singing
You've got em beat
We're on our feet
Its Goal ! Goal ! Goal!

Ok, it helps to know the tune. Luckily the jazz explosion of the 1950s soon brought "Oh When The Saints.." to prominence and the song has been associated with the club ever since.

Staplewood Training Ground

Sponsors - Academy
After the move to St Mary's, Saints academy teams did not share the same sponsors as the senior sides. Firstly Centerprise and latterly Orchard Homes sponsored the youngsters.

Staplewood Training Ground
Up until the 1960s, Southampton, like most clubs, did their training at the ground itself, on the pitch. Soon, however, clubs began to think of the conserving the pitch and base the majority of their training elsewhere, Saints included.

Initially they did some training at the Civil Service ground in Shirley, before moving out to Stoneham Lane and Trojans sports ground. This however, was a temporary stay and by the early 1980s they had taken up residence at one of Southampton University's sports grounds just a little bit further along the road from Trojan's.

This had the added advantage that the youth teams could play there on a Saturday morning, unlike at Trojans, who as a Rugby & Hockey club, had no football pitches. Stoneham had advantages in that it was a private ground with good facilities and offered them a secluded training base, but the fact was the club didn't own it and had no permanent base of their own.

In the 1982 a local businessman called Peter Price pulled a few strings. He'd surprisingly succeeded in getting his Sunday side Road Sea into the Southern League and he built a stadium to that standard at Marchwood, naming the ground Road Sea Park and the team RS Southampton.

For several years they flourished. At one stage they were just one rung below the Conference but the team had few supporters, and as Price lost interest, it started to decline. In 1987 only five years after effectively forming, the team folded leaving Road Sea Park empty.

With the land categorised as green belt, it was not to be sold for housing and within a few years it was purchased by Saints. It was ideal, not only did it have a ready made stadium with seating and floodlights, where youth and reserve team games could be played, but it also had a large field adjacent, that could be used for training sessions.

By the early 1990s, Saints were fully functional in their new training facility and they started to develop it, adding club offices. They also started to play the majority of reserve games there to help preserve The Dell pitch, although they tended to still play the bigger London club sides in the main stadium.

As the millennium arrived, Saints started to expand the facilities further. The biggest development was the building of a massive indoor sports hall complete with Astroturf and a virtually full-sized pitch. The structure also contained facilities for the players to relax in, with lounges containing internet terminals alongside restaurant facilities. Ironically as the club dropped out of the Premier League it could justly claim that in Staplewood, they had a facility the envy of most clubs in the land.

Jim Steele (FA Cup Hero)

Jim joined the Club in January 1972 from Dundee, just in time to suffer in the 0-7 reverse at Leeds United. Over the next few years Jim established himself as a first choice defender forming a solid partnership with Mel Blyth. The 1976 FA Cup final was his greatest game for the club, many newspapers making him their man of the match.

Still only 26 he should have been approaching his peak,

Jim Steele

but the following season would be his last, not only for Saints but in Britain. March 1977 was his final month at the club. It started with him first deflecting the ball into his own net in the FA Cup replay at Old Trafford and then being sent off.

His penultimate game in the Cup Winners Cup quarter final against Anderlecht saw him let a simple through ball slip under his foot to let the Belgians in for a goal that won the tie on aggregate. That was to be his last appearance at The Dell, although he did play on the Saturday away to Nottingham Forest.

It's argued that had Jim's temperament been that little bit better, he could have played another five years and become one of the true Dell legends. He departed for the States, where he would play football and work for the next seventeen years.

He uprooted again and came back to Southampton to run the Chamberlayne Arms pub in Sholing. Latterly he has been running a pub in the Cotswolds.
1972-77. 200 (1) Apps. 1 Goal.

Bobby Stokes (FA Cup Hero)

Everyone at The Dell loved Bobby. Working his way up from the youth ranks he made his debut in 1969 against Burnley, just turned 18. He scored twice and a star was born. It would be a couple of years before he won a regular place.

Bobby worked tirelessly for the side, although often overshadowed by more illustrious names. However his moment of fame nearly never happened. In 1976, he was on the transfer list and Lawrie McMenemy was trying to arrange a swap deal with Portsmouth for Paul Went, but at the last minute Bobby got cold feet. A life-changing decision.

An ever-present in during the FA Cup run, he scored against Blackpool in round 4 and a vital equaliser at West Bromwich Albion in round 5, before his greatest day.

There can't be a Saints fan that doesn't know the build

Bobby Stokes with his golden goal award in 1976

Tragically, after running a pub, then working at his cousin's café in Portsmouth, and the breakdown of his marriage, Bobby passed away in May 1995. Many close to him felt that life for him was never the same after that goal – the greatest goal in the club's history. 1969-77. 238 (26) Apps. 55 Goals.

Substitutes

Substitutes were first allowed in the Football League in season 1965/66 and for the first two seasons were only permitted to be used when a player was injured.

Saints first ever substitute was Ken Wimhurst. He came on after 30 minutes play in the home game with Coventry City on 8th September 1965 when Goalkeeper John Hollowbread sustained a serious knee injury. As he was carried off, Hollowbread was not to know that he would never play League Football again. Although Wimhurst replaced him he did not go between the sticks. This fell to Cliff Huxford who kept a clean sheet, as Saints won 1-0 with a Martin Chivers goal.

In fact it was Chivers who holds the distinction of being the club's first "super sub," coming off the bench to score Saints only goal in a 1-3 reverse against Newcastle United at The Dell, in April 1967.

Saints first ever use of a substitute goalkeeper in a League game came in the 2-0 victory over Everton on 8th October 1994. Bruce Grobbelaar fractured his cheekbone and was replaced by Dave Beasant.

Saints made history at the Millennium Stadium in Cardiff when Paul Jones became the first ever substitute goalkeeper to come on in an FA Cup Final, replacing Antti Niemi who had pulled a calf muscle.

John Sydenham

John Sydenham is perhaps the forgotten man of the club's great teams of the 1950s and 1960s. Many will remember the attacking flair of Paine, Chivers, Davies, Reeves, Channon and even O'Brien. But how many recall John Sydenham?

It's time to put the record straight, because Sydenham

up to the goal, but here it is anyway. 83 minutes are on the clock. A long drop kick from Turner. Osgood tries to flick it on but misses. Channon passes the ball short to McCalliog, who hits a first time pass to find Stokes in the clear. He takes one stride and hits it with his left foot. It doesn't look clean but it stays low and enters the left corner of Stepney's goal. Pandemonium ensues.

After the game a smiling Bobby, holding the Cup told the nation, "I'm off the list." Sadly though he wasn't. In April 1977, after less than a dozen more games for Saints, he left for a spell in the States, before finally getting that move to Fratton Park.

It wasn't the right move, despite being a Pompey lad born and bred. The Fratton faithful could not accept the man who had won the cup for their greatest rivals and within a year he had gone back to the USA. His league career over and he was still only 27.

played a part in the success of all of those players.

Coming from the youth side that did so well in 1956/57, Sydenham was given his first team debut in May 1957, still aged only 17. Along with Terry Paine, he posed a twin winger threat that many teams couldn't come to terms with. Whilst Paine relied on skill, John had blistering pace and in 1959/60 he made England U-23 appearances.

But in July 1960 came a shock. He was called up for National Service, and although he managed to be available for a few games, for the next two seasons his career was on hold. On his demob he was back and as lethal as ever, only missing two games in 1962/63, as Saints prepared for their assault on promotion to the top flight. John was a virtual ever-present for four seasons.

1966 was a momentous year for football. Apart from Saints promotion, England won the World Cup. With changing football tactics, John was often left out of away games in the first three seasons in the top flight.

Sydenham would save his best ever game for one of his last and it couldn't have come at a bigger away game. Saints travelled to Old Trafford in August 1969 and Sydenham murdered United full back Shay Brennan, providing crosses for the first three of Ron Davies' four-goal haul. United were destroyed 4-1. Many considered it John Sydenham's finest hour for the club, but less than four months later he would have played his last game still aged only 30.

Many would say that he retired too early, certainly those that attended a game at the Dell in 1973 to see an ex-Saints XI take on their Le Havre counterparts thought that at 33, he still had the pace for First Division football. In his time at The Dell, Sydenham scored 40 goals, but he laid on countless more.

Despite having lived in Australia for the past two decades, he is always back at the club when there is a special occasion. At a dinner for the Ted Bates Trust in 2005, he donated the match ball used in the demolition of Manchester City in the FA Cup in 1960. The ball went into a charity auction to raise money for a statue to his former manager.
1957-69. 401(1) Apps. 40 Goals.

T
Testimonials
Over the years there have been many testimonials for Saints players but three in particular will always stick in the memory of the supporters, for several reasons. Firstly each of the trio was considered a local boy made good, despite the fact that only one was Southampton born; secondly because, for varying reasons, each game was a sell out – a rarity for a testimonial; and thirdly, well, each game was different.

Mick Channon Testimonial v. QPR. May 3rd 1976. By pure luck, Mick Channon had scheduled his testimonial match on May 3rd. Initially it looked to be just another Monday night end-of-season game, albeit against a QPR side who arrived knowing that the following night they could be crowned League Champions if Liverpool lost at Wolves. (They didn't and QPR finished runners-up.) However, when Saints got through to the FA Cup Final on May 1st, things changed.

By the afternoon of the game, the city had been in a state of euphoria for two days, with only stand seats sold in advance. By 5pm. The Dell was under siege, as everyone wanted to acclaim the Cup winners - even though 200,000 had turned out the day before.

An hour before the kick-off and the gates were locked. The official attendance was 29,508, but fans were climbing in, bribing stewards, in fact doing anything to get in. It's generally regarded as the record attendance at the ground, with fans sitting on the roof and even on the perimeter track.

The team came out to a deafening roar. Bobby Stokes was presented with a car for scoring the winner on Saturday, despite the fact he couldn't drive and the team did a lap of honour. In truth it was played with

The biggest pitch invasion ever? Saints fans come off the terraces at the Mick Channon Testimonial in 1976 - thought to be the biggest attendance at The Dell

more gusto than games are these days and as it entered the last phase it was 2-2, Stokes scoring both of course.

But the crowd was restless. More and more were encroaching onto the pitch and when a goal-bound shot from Peter Osgood hit a spectator and went in, the referee blew for full time, prompting the biggest pitch invasion ever seen, as fans locked outside flooded in to join the fun.

Francis Benali. Current Squad v. Ex-Saints. 13th May 1997.

Saints had just escaped relegation and the fans were in good spirits. It meant that all 15,200 tickets were snapped up well before the day of the game, to honour a player who as the fans appreciated, wasn't the most gifted but was certainly the most committed. Benali for his part, wanted to make it a night to remember and conscious that modern day testimonials often have the

Francis Benali is acclaimed by the loyal Saints supporters at his testimonial

footballing excitement of watching paint dry, decided it would be part pantomime part football match, but mainly pantomime.

No one can remember the exact score, although the official statistics are 8-7 to the Ex-Saints. Benali scored his first-ever goal for the first team, with his right foot of all things, and it was a 25-yard screamer past Tim Flowers.

Unofficial scorers had the result as 15 all, it was all so confusing as to which goals counted and which didn't.

Dave Beasant revelled in an outfield role that involved him walking the ball into the net whilst his team-mates surrounded him preventing the opposition tackling him. Other highlights were Le Tissier playing in goal and fighting a personal duel with Shearer, desperate to score and surprisingly winning.

It was a feel-good night that the fans enjoyed far more than seeing a few pros knocking the ball around with little interest. Luckily over the years, Saints have been blessed with enough old boys with a sense of humour and personality to match.

Matthew Le Tissier. 14th May 2002. v. England XI.
Another night in the Benali mould. Le God had retired and St Mary's was packed to the rafters to praise the Lord. The England team included Alan Shearer, Kevin Keegan, Peter Beardsley, Chris Waddle and Paul Gascoigne, such as the affection that he was held in the footballing world.

The game ended nine apiece. Matt of course, scored, as did his two brothers for the home side, whilst his son Mitchell got four for the England XI, with allegations of match fixing going around the ground. Luckiest fan in the ground was an unnamed ball boy given a shirt by Kevin Keegan and sent on to score for Saints.

At the end, a collection of Matt's greatest goals were shown on the big screens whilst Frank Sinatra or somebody just like him, sang "My Way."

Le Tissier, clearly choked with the occasion bowed out, thanking his family and the fans, who he said, were the reason he stayed with one club throughout his career: "As the song says, I did it my way, but I like to think I did it your way too." There was barely a dry eye in the house.

Testimonials Home, Post War

Ron Reynolds	v. Chelsea 29/04/64 won 3-2
John Hollowbread	v. Portsmouth 10/05/66 won 6-1
Tommy Traynor	v. Twente Enschede 31/10/66 drew 3-3
John Sydenham	v. Portsmouth 20/04/70 lost 2-4
Ted Bates	v. Leeds United 14/08/74 drew 1-1
Terry Paine	v. Ipswich Town 29/04/75 drew 1-1
Mick Channon	v. QPR 03/05/76 drew 2-2
Lawrie McMenemy	v. Nottingham Forest 11/05/79 lost 0-4
George Horsfall	v. Glasgow Rangers 16/05/82 won 4-2
Nick Holmes	v. Benfica 05/08/86 won 4-1
Steve Mills Leukemia Fund	v. All Star 23/03/88 won 7-3
Francis Benali	v. Ex-Saints 13/05/97 lost 7-8
Jason Dodd	v. Woggy's Wanderers 22/05/01 lost 1-3
Matthew Le Tissier	v. England XI 14/05/02 drew 9-9
Danny Wallace	v. All Stars 17/05/04 drew 2-2

Time Gentlemen Please

In the days before footballers never had to work again after their first season, it was a time-honoured tradition that ex-players would become publicans. Here are some Saints who have run pubs in and around the city.

Reuben Agboola
For many years in the nineties, Reuben was the landlord of The Sporting View bar, more commonly known as the Pub in the park at Southampton Sports Centre.

Bryn Elliott
Not really a pub, but after retiring, Bryn ran an off licence in Millbrook Road East for many years.

Charlie George
After giving up playing, Charlie took over the running of a pub in the town of New Milton in the New Forest.

John Hollowbread
After injury cut his career short, John took over the Sun Inn at Romsey.

Ted McDougall
After finishing his playing career with a spell in the USA, Ted returned and took over the Mill Arms at Dunbridge just outside Romsey. In 1980/81 season he turned out regularly for the pub's Sunday morning side, the same season he had started playing for Blackpool.

George O'Brien
George was for many years, the landlord at the Waterloo Arms in Waterloo Road in Freemantle. He then moved to Scotland in 1990 before returning to the city to become a taxi driver.

Peter Rodrigues
When he retired from the game in 1977

Advertisement for Peter Rodriguez's pub

"Pedro" took over the King Rufus at Eling. Pride of place behind the bar was a big portrait of that day at Wembley. After a spell in Wales he returned to Southampton and became the steward at the Conservative Club in Angelsea Road, Shirley.

Jim Steele
After returning to the UK in the mid 1990s, Jim ran the Chamberlayne Arms in Sholing for a time, until moving to the Cotswolds to run a pub there.

Eric Webber
After a long league career, followed by a stint managing Poole Town, Eric packed in football to take over The Manor House pub in Woolston in 1970, spending 14 years as mine host.

Transfer Fees
Top Ten Fees Paid Out
£4 m. Rory Delap (Derby County) August 2001
£3.5 m. Agustin Delgado (Necaxa, Mexico) November 2001
£3.5 m. Kevin Phillips (Sunderland) August 2003
£2.5 m. David Prutton (Nottingham Forest) January 2003
£2.1 m. Nigel Quashie Portsmouth January 2005
£2 m. Peter Crouch (Aston Villa) 2004
£2 m. Antti Niemi (Hearts) 2002
£2 m. Michael Svensson (Troyes) 2002
£2 m. David Hirst (Sheffield Wednesday) 1997
£1.75 m. Brett Ormerod (Blackpool) 2001

Top Five Transfer Fees Received
£12 m.Theo Walcott (Arsenal) January 2006 (£5 million down, £5 million based on appearances, £2 Million based on England caps)
£10 m. Gareth Bale (Tottenham Hotspur) May 2007 (£5 million down, £5 million based on appearances)
£8.2 m. Dean Richards (Tottenham Hotspur) September 2001

£7.5 m. Kevin Davies (Blackburn Rovers) May 1998
£7 m. Wayne Bridge (Chelsea) (plus Graeme Le Saux)

Tommy Traynor
Its easy to trace Tommy's career. He only had one League club and that was Southampton. He arrived from Dundalk, Eire in the summer of 1952 and would spend over 13 years at the club, playing his last game in the club's promotion season of 1965/66. Along the way, he became the club's record appearance holder for the time.

The left back was also capped eight times by his country between 1954 and 1964. Famed for his fearless sliding tackles and tactical know-how, he had a great left foot.

Not only was Tommy a one club man, he never left his adopted city. On retiring he ran an off licence then worked in Southampton docks and was instrumental in the running of the city's premier youth football set up, The Tyro League.

Annti Niemi

Tommy was due to be presented with a gold watch in February 1964, before the match against Portsmouth, to mark his 500th appearance for the club (including friendlies).

A spanner was thrown in the works when the midweek game against Swansea was postponed. The club, keen to honour Tommy, decided to press ahead with the ceremony despite the fact that he was technically only making his 499th appearance. 1952-65. 487 Apps. 8 Goals.

Tribute That Never Happened
With the recent coverage of the Ted Bates Statue fiasco and its subsequent removal, it's interesting to note that this isn't the first time that an attempted tribute has hit the buffers.Many older Saints supporters will recall that Ted, arguably the greatest

See you again soon

Flyer advertising the Ted Bates tribute

manager in the club's history, had a testimonial against Leeds United in August 1974. But the truth is the original game was scheduled for 30th April 1974, against old rivals Portsmouth. We can only speculate as to why this game didn't go ahead. Certainly it was advertised in the programme versus Manchester United ten days prior to the date. Somewhere along the line it was called off at short notice.

Its not too hard to hazard a guess why. Saints were heading towards relegation in that season and perhaps it was felt that a testimonial only three days after the final game of the season wouldn't be great timing.

In addition it was probably felt that Saints relegation would attract a large number of Pompey fans along to gloat. With all this in mind, the decision was taken to postpone the game to another date and different opponents.

Ian Turner (FA Cup Hero)

Ian Turner followed his old boss Lawrie McMenemy from Grimsby Town and arrived on the south coast just in time to make four appearances in goal as the club slipped into the Second Division in 1974. He couldn't quite find the consistency to make the number one jersey his own. In fact he started the FA Cup winning

season in the reserves, as Steve Middleton played the first 17 games. But Turner won his place back in November and was ever-present thereon. Almost a third of his career appearances with Saints were made in that glorious 1975/76 season.

His best game in the FA Cup run came at Bradford City where he kept a clean sheet and even produced a save that was voted one of the saves of the season on BBC Match of the Day. In the run up to the final, Manchester United made no secret of the fact that they considered Turner the weak link and intended to put him under pressure.

Watching the opening minutes of the final is still a

Ian Turner

harrowing experience. Ian's first action saw him fail to hold a Gordon Hill shot, but luckily he was fouled as he attempted to retrieve it. His second save was similar.

He couldn't hold the ball, and things looked bad for Saints. They had a keeper with the jitters. But things changed as the game went on. Hill was played through, but Turner was alert to the situation got there first to hook it away. His nerves were calmed and he would look solid thereafter. This gave Saints confidence. The keeper had weathered the storm and came through.

After the Final, Turner's Saints career was all but over. He would play just four games the following season, 12 in the promotion year, with his final game coming in February 1978. He stayed at the club until January 1979, alternating games in the reserves with spells out on loan. He was another Cup Final hero whose league career was over long before 30.

Turner remained living in the area while working in the oil industry, before taking a job in Essex in 2003. He always attends Cup Final reunions.
1974-79. 107 Apps.

U
UEFA CUP

This competition was originally called the Inter City Fairs Cup and Saints first qualified in 1969, beating Rosenborg away 1-0, following it up with a 2-0 home victory in front of 22,329. The attendance was only a few short of that season's average. Vitoria Guimaraes were dispatched in the second round 8-4 on aggregate after a 3-3 draw in Portugal and an emphatic 5-1 win at the Dell.

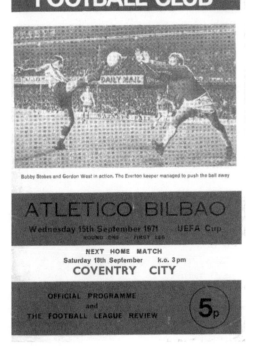

SOUTHAMPTON FOOTBALL CLUB

Bobby Stokes and Gordon West in action. The Everton keeper managed to push the ball away

ATLETICO BILBAO
Wednesday 15th September 1971   UEFA Cup
ROUND ONE — FIRST LEG

NEXT HOME MATCH
Saturday 18th September   k.o. 3pm
COVENTRY CITY

OFFICIAL PROGRAMME
and
THE FOOTBALL LEAGUE REVIEW   **5p**

Hopes of an exotic trip to somewhere near the Med were dashed when Saints were drawn to play Newcastle United in the third round. A scoreless draw at St James Park was a good result but lacked the vital away goal. Saints paid the price when Pop Robson equalised an early Mick Channon goal with six minutes remaining, to send the Geordies through on away goals. They would eventually win the competition itself.

Two years later, in 1971, Saints found themselves in the inaugural season of the newly named UEFA Cup, basically the same competition with a different name

A tough tie against Atletico Bilbao came out of the hat. It was fitting that the two teams should face each other.

Bilbao were founded by exiles from Britain and allegedly play in red and white stripes because many of the founders were from ports such as Southampton. (They reverted to the original name Athletic Bilbao in 1977.) Saints took a 2-1 lead at The Dell, but went out after a 0-2 defeat in Spain.

It would be another ten years before Saints would play in the competition again. (A Cup Winners Cup campaign had been sandwiched in between). In the first round, Saints played Limerick United.

A full house in the west of Ireland appreciated a visiting side that contained four England captains, plus one other full cap (David Armstrong), two Under-21 caps, one Yugoslavian international and only three players with no International honours, a mean feat back in those days. Southampton took a 3-0 lead back to England, after goals by Steve Moran (2) and Armstrong.

Surprisingly, a fortnight later at The Dell the same side could only manage a 1-1 draw but that was enough. Kevin Keegan scored the goal. In the 2nd round Sporting Lisbon arrived at The Dell and shocked the home fans by taking a 0-3 half time lead. Saints rallied to pull two goals back but a last minute effort made it 2-4 on the night to the Portuguese. It was too much even for the free scoring Saints, who missed a few chances as Sporting were content to sit back on their advantage. The return leg finished 0-0 and the campaign was over.

The following season saw Saints draw Norrkoping of Sweden in the 1st round and Saints fans could be forgiven for thinking this would be easy. Those ideas were dispelled when the part timers came to the Dell and earned a 2-2 draw. It could have been worse. Only a last gasp Mark Wright header ensuring the tie was at least even going to the second leg.

In Sweden it was a disaster, although it was a only a scoreless draw, sending Saints out on goal difference. Saints dominated the game and should have gone through, but worse was to follow. Saints players Steve Moran and Mark Wright were arrested and held in Sweden accused of sexual assault after a night of high jinks at the team hotel.

Both were soon released as the charges were proved to have no grounds, but they were still in custody when Saints beat Notts County at The Dell on the Saturday.

In 1985/86, Saints once again qualified, but found themselves banned from the competition as UEFA issued a blanket ban to all English clubs from competing in Europe due to the events at the European Cup Final at Heysel.

Saints qualified for the 2003/04 competition by way of meeting Arsenal in the FA Cup Final. Usually it would be the winners who would go through, but because the Gunners had already qualified for the Champions League, Saints took their place. In the 1st round Steau Bucharest visited St Mary's for its first European tie. In front of 30,557, it wasn't to be the result that most of the crowd wanted. Trailing 0-1 at half time Saints equalised through Kevin Phillips, but they couldn't get a second.

Bucharest was invaded by over 3,000 Saints supporters, the biggest away following ever to go to Romania, including International games and visits from the likes of Liverpool. Steau, knowing they had the away goal, stood firm. With ten minutes remaining, Phillips should have won the game, when clean through. As Saints pushed, Steau nicked a goal against the run of play. Saints most recent European tour was over.

The Ugly Inside

Although it can't claim to be the first Saints fanzine, The Ugly Inside is the Godfather of them all. The Ugly, as it became known, first hit the streets on the 30th April 1988, prior to the home game against West Ham United. It sold 250 copies, a decent first result. The following season it adopted its trademark cover and campaigned for Saints to return to a traditional striped kit. Someone was listening as in 1989 the club did just that. Someone was reading as well and in its heyday of 1989-95 it would regularly sell over 2,500 copies per issue, one edition reaching a remarkable 3,500.

In the early days the emphasis was on humour but as the years went by it became more of a campaigning fanzine. Its two co-founders helped to form the Southampton Independent Supporters Association and it lead from the front when tackling anything from the Stoneham Stadium situation to the alleged dodgy share dealings which saw Rupert Lowe's arrival at the club in the reverse takeover.

By the year 2000 The Ugly found itself in a waning fanzine marketplace as the internet came into vogue and in August of that year it converted to a webzine. It has remained a staple of the internet ever since. www.theuglyinside.net

Undefeated

Saints have only gone one whole season undefeated at home in the Football League. This was in their second season in the League ranks in 1921-22, when they won the Third Division (S) Championship. This included their longest unbeaten home run of 31 games which stretched from 21st January 1921 until 28th August 1922, when Leeds United won 0-2 at the Dell.

This was a golden period, as from 5th September 1921 Saints put together their best undefeated spell in total, 19 games up until January 14th and a one goal defeat at Brentford.

Saints longest undefeated run away from home is nine games and this was achieved in two seasons, 1949/50 and also 1977/78.

Up The Middle For Charlie

Charlie Wayman was perhaps the first Dell superstar after joining the club from Newcastle United in October 1947 for a club record fee of £10,000. The former miner came to bolster the promotion push. Unfortunately, despite scoring 17 goals in 27 games, Charlie couldn't get Saints up as they finished agonisingly third, but a cult had been born.

Charlie Wayman

The following season and "Up the middle for Charlie" was the cry from the terraces and more often that not Wayman would oblige, latching on to the through ball and with a swing of his left foot, a goal would often be the result.

For the next two seasons Charlie reigned supreme. In his first full season he hit 32 from 37 league games. His last goal came with seven games to go, the only goal in a win at promotion rivals Spurs. The trouble was that Wayman had been a passenger for most of the second half injuring a thigh muscle before scoring the 82nd minute winner with his injured leg. This of course was in the days before substitutes.

With only seven games left, the team was eight points clear. A mammoth gap with only two points for a win, but without Wayman, Saints would falter. The seven games saw only one win and four defeats as the goals dried up, scoring only two. Wayman would be brought back, clearly still not fit, to no avail. Saints finished third again, losing out by one point.

In 1949/50 Southampton were once again favourites for promotion and Charlie was fit, scoring 24 goals in 36 games. This time Saints suffered no run-in nerves winning six and drawing three of their final nine games. But it was not to be enough as they lost out on goal difference to both the Sheffield sides, all three finishing on 52 points. Wednesday had the better margin. It must have been a rough night in Sheffield that night.

By then Charlie was a legend. The Charlie Wayman café, despite being nothing to do with him was packed and fans looked forward to 1950/51 with relish. Little did they know he had played his last game for the club. His wife had not settled in the south and he requested a transfer. Saints decided not to stand in his way and in September 1950 he moved to Preston North End for £10,000 plus Eddy Brown.

Even to this day Wayman is revered by Saints fans, most of whom never saw him play. His goals to game ratio is the best of any regular Saints striker.

Charlie eventually retired back to his native North East to work in the brewery industry, sadly passing away in February 2006. Southampton paid tribute to him and to Peter Osgood with a moving round of applause before the home match against Coventry City on March 4th, 2006.
1947-50. 107 Apps. 77 Goals.

Up & Under
When Leicester City visited the Dell in October 1967, Saints fans had reason to be optimistic. After all they hadn't been beaten at The Dell in the League all season and the beaten teams had included three of the eventual top four, including eventual champions Manchester City, who had been dispatched 3-2.

Leicester lined up with future Saint Peter Shilton in goal. Even at 18 he was considered so good that Leicester had sold Gordon Banks, England's World Cup winning keeper and world number one at that time.

The game started well for Saints with Ron Davies scoring just before the half hour, but on the stroke of half time the Foxes equalised and then it went all wrong.

With barely 20 minutes of the second period gone, the visitors were 1-3 up and had the game won, but worse was to come. If Sinclair's goal to give Leicester a three goal cushion in the 88th minute was enough to make fans stream to the exits those that got there quickly were to witness a rare event: a goal from a goalkeeper.

Campbell Forsyth

As Shilton prepared to launch the ball up field in the final minute, nothing more can have been on his mind other that putting it into the opponents half and running the clock down. Was it the wind that caught it? Even Shilton himself called it a complete fluke, as it bounced on the edge of the area catching out Saints keeper Campbell Forsyth, flying over him for the fifth and final goal in a 1-5 drubbing.

Campbell Forsyth should have been destined for a long career as Sir Alex Ferguson's life coach. The freak goal wasn't his bad judgement, he said. No, it was the lines!

Groundsman Len Stansbridge was a known perfectionist, so much so, that he actually hand-painted the lines on the pitch. Forsyth claimed this gave them a hard baked effect, so when the ball hit them, it literally shot past the goalie at a completely different height than he would have expected. Mmm.

Sadly for Forsyth a video exists that dispels this theory and disputes the fact that the ball bounced anywhere near the line, leaving poor old Campbell well and truly in the soup.

V

The Valley Slags

The Valley Slags came to prominence in the summer of 1995 when they released their single "The Legend of a Saint," dedicated to Matt Le Tissier, which soon became a hit in the local charts.

The group's fifteen minutes of fame came when they were invited to perform, or rather mime, the song prior to the Leeds United game at The Dell in August 1995. Then, as now, Leeds travelling support had somewhat of a reputation, so from the opening chords of the song, abuse was hurled at the group. They gamely continued on.

However, as the lead singer, in possession of a live microphone, moved closer to the away section, the abuse became a little more personal. Stewards suddenly noticed that an incident might take place. They pounced on the singer and bundled him away from the Leeds section.

In the middle of the melee, the mic was still switched on and the crowd were treated to a live performance of grunting and swearing by both the stewards and the singer. The hilarious incident made the national papers and football magazines, and in fairness didn't do any harm to the sales of the record.

Various Odds & Ends

Southampton's third round FA Cup tie against York City in the big freeze of 1963 was postponed nine times, before finally being played on February 13th with Saints winning 5-0. This was the first game Saints had completed since Boxing Day, although one fixture against Charlton Athletic at the Valley did get started but was abandoned after 19 minutes in the middle of a blizzard.

●●●

Saints have scored one hundred goals in a league season on three occasions. In 1957/58 they hit 112 as they finished sixth in Division Three (S). Two years later in 1959/60 they won the same division, hitting 106 goals along the way, and then in 1963/64 they hit exactly 100 scoring six on the final day against Rotherham United.

In each of those seasons their goals against column was almost as bad, 72 in 1957/58, 75 in 1959/60 and 73 in 1963/64. That meant that in each of those seasons an average of 4 goals was scored in every match.

●●●

As Saints headed for their third Southern League title in a row in 1898/99 they travelled to arch rivals Millwall on 26th November. With Saints leading 4-1 the referee blew for full time early, only to get back to the dressing rooms to realise his mistake. He tried to bring the teams back on to complete the match but the crowd, as volatile then as they are now, had invaded the pitch and refused to leave.

The final ten minutes were played on 12th April 1899 prior to a Western league meeting between the sides. But to the relief of the players the venue was The Dell and not The Den.

●●●

The Dell pitch used to be one of the smallest in the League measuring only 110 yards long by 72 yards wide. This was about as big as it could get with the perimeter fencing being only a yard or two from the touchline. The move to St Mary's allowed the club to increase the size to 115 yards by 75 yards.

●●●

Since joining the Football League in 1920, Saints have met non league opponents in the FA Cup on six occasions. Luckily they have only been beaten on the one occasion, the first in 1938/39 when they lost at home to Chelmsford City 1-4.

In a five-year spell in the 1950s, as the club festered in the Third Division (S), they met non league opposition four times. Barnet were beaten in London 4-1 in 1954/55. Two years later in 1956/57 it was a south coast derby in the second round, as Weymouth came to The Dell and were narrowly beaten 3-2.

In 1957/58 it was the turn of Walton & Hersham, beaten 6-1at the Dell, and then finally in 1958/59, Woking were beaten 4-1 again at the Dell. Its been nearly fifty years since Saints last met non league opposition and seven decades since they have lost. Is it about time that fate dealt the club a potential banana skin?

•••

In the 1947/48 season Saints central defender Eric Day became the proud father of a baby boy and vowed that he would name him after the next Saint to score. On 6th March August Fisher Scott, to give him his full title, duly obliged against Coventry City. Day, presumably under severe pressure from his wife, reneged on the promise.

•••

Many Saints fan assume that Saints have worn black shorts since Victorian times, but this isn't quite true. In fact up until the 1950s Saints shorts were a very dark blue before changing to the black we all know so well.

What isn't so well known is that in 2001 Saints almost changed the home shorts to white. Manager Glenn Hoddle, an advocate of sport psychology, decided that white shorts were far better at putting opponents at a disadvantage.

The club even went as far as running up a few pairs for the manager to examine. The idea was shelved after Hoddle's abrupt departure. Perhaps, though, there was something in Hoddle's thinking. When Saints met Watford in the FA Cup semi final in 2003, their shirts didn't clash, but the black shorts did.

The simple solution was for Saints to play in white

shorts and the Hoddle models were retrieved from the back of a cupboard at the training ground. They must have worked, as Saints won.

•••

Until the game between Portsmouth and Reading in September 2007, which finished 7-4, Saints were involved in two matches that had the highest all-time aggregate scores in the Premiership:
Southampton 6, Manchester United.3. Oct. 26, 1996.
Tottenham 7, Southampton 2. March 11, 2000.

•••

The most recent 5-5 draw in the top division was also a Southampton game. v. Coventry City. May 4, 1982. (Division 1)

•••

Saints players feature a lot in the Most League appearances (all time list, all clubs):
1st Peter Shilton.   1005 apps. (Leicester, Stoke, Forest Southampton, Derby, Plymouth, Bolton, Leyton O.)
3rd Terry Paine.   824 apps. (Southampton, Hereford)
8th Dave Beasant (right). 777 apps. (Wimbledon, Newcastle, Grimsby, Wolves, Chelsea, Southampton, Nottm. Forest, Portsmouth, Brighton.)

Other players in the list:
Frank Worthington.757 apps. (11 clubs) (34 apps. Southampton)
Alan Ball.   743 apps. (5 clubs)
Mick Mills.   732 apps. (3 clubs)
Mike Channon.   718 apps. (6 clubs)
Glenn Cockerill.   714 apps. (7 clubs)
John Burridge.   691 apps. (15 clubs)

•••

In 2004 Southampton's Dave Roberts was named as *"IOG Saltex* Groundsman of the Year" for the best pitch in the League, at St. Mary's.

•••

Carlton Palmer was sent off for each of his five premiership clubs: Sheffield Wednesday, Leeds United, Southampton, Nottingham Forest, Coventry City.

•••

During the 1986-87 season, Eric Nixon played in four Divisions in one season: Manchester City and Southampton (Div.1), Bradford City (2), Carlisle United (3), and Wolverhampton Wanderers (4).

Victories
Victories In A Season- Highest
Saints won 26 of their forty-six games in the 3rd Division Championship season of 1960/61, the clubs highest number so far.

Victories In A Season- Lowest
Saints won only six games in season 1969/70 although luckily enough this was still enough to save them from relegation. No such luck though in the club's last Premiership season when they equalled this unwanted record and were relegated, although in fairness this was in only 38 games as opposed to the 42 played in 69/70. See also Wins

W
Wallace Brothers
The first of the three brothers to sign for Saints was Danny Wallace, who became the club's youngest debutant at the time when he made his debut, still an apprentice aged 16 years and 313 days old.

He went on to become a Saints regular, becoming the first player to score in a live televised game at The Dell against Liverpool in 1984. He was a one cap England wonder scoring on his one and only game against Egypt in 1986.

Soon after this he was joined at the club by twin brothers Rodney and Raymond, five years younger than Danny. They had the distinction of becoming the first trio of brothers to play in the same league side since the 1920s when they lined up against Sheffield Wednesday on October 22nd 1988.

They would not stay together for long however. In all they only made 25 appearances as a trio. A year later Danny was sold to Manchester United for a record fee of £1.2 million.

However the other two had ideas above their station and became unsettled. In truth Rodney, an attacking wide man was a great player, but Raymond couldn't get in the side. In his last six months at The Dell, in the summer of 1991, they both went to Leeds United for a combined fee set by a tribunal of only £1.6 million. Ray's £100k valuation in that figure was considered generous by some.

Sadly Danny's career petered out at Manchester United. It was later discovered that he had contracted multiple sclerosis. In May 2004, despite his other former clubs making the right noises, Saints became the only one to do anything concrete for Danny, when they held a testimonial game for him at St Mary's.

A lingering bitterness towards the twins for the manner of their leaving and the fact that Danny had played only one game at the Dell for United since his departure, meant younger fans had no real memories of him. It kept the attendance down to a lower figure than it should have been.

In 2006 Danny bravely completed the London marathon in five and a half days to raise funds towards MS. He was presented his medal by boxer Michael Thomas who was the inspiration to Danny having completed the same course in 2003. Danny Wallace won one England cap and is the second shortest ever England player (5'4").

Danny Wallace 299 appearances (+ 18 sub) 79 goals

The Wallace brothers, Rod, Danny and Ray

Rodney Wallace 132 Appearances (+ 19 sub) 56 goals
Raymond Wallace 44 Appearances (+2 sub) 0 goals

Charlie Wayman
See Up The Middle for Charlie.

Len Wilkins
Probably not the first name to trip off the tongues of
Saints supporters, but with 275 games to his name at

his hometown club, Len Wilkin's story is one that
deserves to be remembered.

Spotted playing on the Common, in the same side as
ex-Saints Arthur Holt, Len Wilkins spent three seasons
at The Dell before breaking into the side at 23. He
spent ten years as a first team regular, many as
captain. He was nicknamed Spud due to his fondness
for potatoes. Len decided to retire and emigrate to
Canada and his last game for the club was at home to

Watford in April 1958. It was an emotional occasion. He received a rousing reception as he walked to the centre circle to toss the coin for the last time and the band joined in as the crowd spontaneously broke into a rendition of Auld Lang Syne.

That wasn't the end of Len Wilkins and football. In Canada he was soon involved in the development of the sport in that country, playing for various sides including a stint in Los Angeles, where he represented California against Manchester United in 1960. On his return to Ontario he continued to play football in local leagues, turning out in goal at the ripe old age of 73. He was a familiar figure in his local park where he would often sport a Saints shirt. Always a visitor to The Dell when he returned periodically to Southampton, sadly Len passed away in 2003. 1948-58. 275 Apps. 3 Goals.

Wins
Saints biggest wins:
11-0	v. Northampton T. 28 December 1901 (Southern Lge)	
11-0	v. Watford. 13 December 1902 (Southern League)	
8-0	v. Northampton Town. 24 December 1921	
9-3	v. Wolverhampton Wanderers. 18 September 1965	
8-2	v. Coventry City. 28 April 1984	
7-1	v. Ipswich Town. 7 January 1961 (FA Cup)	
6-0	v. Luton Town. 8 February 1995 (FA Cup replay)	
6-0	v. Wolverhampton Wanderers. 31 March 2007	

(Championship)
See also Victories

The Wit & Wisdom Of Rupert Lowe
"I'm always sincere even when I'm lying." *Rupert shows that a career in car sales awaits.*

"The problem with supporters is that they don't look at balance sheets only league tables" *Rupert to a bemused fans forum.*

"We will not be pushed around by a bunch of North London Yobbos" *Rupert is not impressed by Spurs attempt to prise Dean Richards away from the Dell.*

"I liken the current situation to that of the Starship Enterprise. The shields are up and the Klingons are shooting at us and every time they land a punch they are sapping our power." *Rupert feels that the supporters are doing the club's chances no good by moaning*

"We want him to stay as long as possible but I cannot give any copper-bottomed answers and say he will be here for the next five years, or two years, or whatever." *Rupert Lowe tries to keep fans sweet while simultaneously slapping a 'for sale' sign across teenage starlet Theo Walcott's forehead.*

"Corruptissima republica plurimae leges (the most corrupt republics have the most laws)" - *Rupert protests in his programme notes at how the finances of England's Premier League, the most successful in Europe, are being threatened by the officials of Mario Monti, Brussels's competition commissioner. (Taken from Roman Historian Tacitus)*

Stan Woodhouse
Joining the Club in 1924 from Bury, Stan went on to make 366 appearances for the club scoring 6 goals from the half back position.

He was very much an unsung hero in his dozen years at the Dell. At the time only Bert Shelley had made more appearances during Saints first half century of existence.

On departing from Milton Road, Stan played non league for Basingstoke before becoming mine host at the Brickmakers Arms in Shirley Warren. In 1951/52 he made a brief return to The Dell as A & B team trainer. Stan died in Southampton in 1977, aged 78. 1924-36. 366 Apps. 6 Goals.

Worst Start
Saints worst ever start to a season in any division came in 1998/99 when they failed to win any of their opening nine games, losing seven and drawing two.

They finally broke their duck with a 2-1 home win against fellow strugglers Coventry City, more than two months after the season had started.

Worthless Cups

Tennent- Caledonian Cup 1976-78

After winning the FA Cup in 1976, Saints were invited to participate in this pre-season tournament held at hosts Glasgow Rangers' Ibrox Stadium. After defeating Manchester City in the semi finals, on the toss of a coin, after the penalty shoot out finished 11-11, Saints met Rangers in the final. They beat them 2-1 with goals from Channon and Peach.

Channon was booed by the home crowd every time he touched the ball after comments made a few months earlier when he had scored England's consolation goal in a 1-2 defeat to Scotland at Hampden Park when he'd said, "The only good thing to come out of Scotland is the road to England."

A year later Saints were again participants, this time they lost to Rangers in the Semi 1-3. Peach scored again. However they defeated St Mirren 2-1 for the third place play off with goals from Alan Ball and Peter Osgood.

Saints final appearance in this tournament came in 1978 when they beat West Bromwich Albion on penalties in the semi final after a Phil Boyer goal saw the game end 1-1. But Saints lost 1-4 to Rangers in the final, Ted McDougall scoring the consolation in his home country.

Patrick Trophy

When Saints signed up to kit manufacturer Patrick in 1980 they agreed to enter the Patrick Cup. Basically this was between Saints and Swansea, another club wearing the French company's gear. Saints went down to the Vetch Field in Wales with all guns blazing winning 5-0, through Steve Moran (2) Boyer, Hebberd & Williams.

X
X-Rated Tackles

Saints have had a few players who have committed fouls on the pitch that shouldn't have been allowed to have been seen by anyone under 18. Perhaps the daddy of them all came at Wimbledon on 17th March 1980

and resulted in one of the eleven red cards that Francis Benali received in his career.

Franny wasn't a dirty player though you could say he was prone to the red mist every now and then. That sometimes resulted in a little bit of retribution dealt to the opposition and this match at Plough Lane was one such occasion.

Six of the Saints side that day were 21 or younger. While some of the main the crazy gang protagonists had left, John Fashanu was till there. However he hadn't reckoned on the strength of Benali. The offence happened in the 59th minute of the game. Grown men turned away as the two competed for a ball on the half way line.

In went the Saints man and up went Fashanu, somersaulting over Benali to hit the floor with a thump. It was an inevitable red card, but it sparked the Saints revival by knocking the wind out of Fashanu and strengthening the resolve of the ten men, who fought back for a 3-3 draw.

Xmas Fixtures

Saints played their first ever game on Christmas Day away to West ham United in 1902/03 season and it suited them, coming home 2-1 victors. When they joined the Football League in 1920 it became normal practice to play the same side home and away on Xmas and Boxing Day/St. Stephens Day. In their inaugural season Saints drew 1-1 with Luton Town away on the 25th followed by the same scoreline the following day.

Perhaps the most difficult trip came two years later when Saints had to travel to Hull City on Xmas Day where they won 3-1. Both teams rushed back to make the Boxing Day kick off at The Dell, when Saints completed the double, this time 2-1.

The records show that for some teams seasonal results went from one extreme to another, winning heavily in the first game only to suffer a steep reverse only a day later. For Saints however, things remained pretty constant. The biggest swing coming in season 30/31 when after winning 3-1 at White Hart Lane on Xmas Day, Saints could have been forgiven for thinking that Boxing Day would be a stroll. They were wrong as Spurs hit three without a reply from the home side.

Saints last ever game on Christmas day was in 1958 when they travelled to Newport County and lost 2-4.

Perhaps the quirkiest Christmas fact of all though, is the run of fixtures played on the Boxing Day, starting in 1898/99 season. Saints hosted Spurs ten seasons in a row on Boxing Day, before Spurs, possibly fed up with such monotony, left the Southern League to become one of the few southern teams in the Football League. It could also have been due to the fact that they lost six of the ten fixtures, drawing three and managing only one win.

Y

Yesterdays Hero
Yesterdays Hero was a 1979 film starring Ian McShane, Adam Faith and Paul Nicholas, from an original screenplay by Jackie Collins. McShane played Rod Turner, an alcoholic washed-up footballer who is signed up to a struggling team in the hope he will rediscover past glories.

Rather than use actors playing in the matches, McShane's team were called the Saints and footage of him in his football kit were interspersed with action from some of Saints matches in the 1978/79 season, mainly the League Cup Final at Wembley against Nottingham Forest.

Saints fans featured strongly in the footage from Wembley, so if you were there, you might be in the movie. Nick Holmes is shown from afar, as McShane supposedly scores the winner in the final. Sadly the film won no Oscars and rarely crops up on TV.

Youth Cup
Although Saints have reached the FA Youth Cup semi final on several occasions, they have only reached the final once, in season 2004/05, when they faced Ipswich Town. Southampton lost in a two legged final, with a 2-2 draw at home and a narrow defeat 0-1 to a late goal, at Portman Road.

Saints first reached the semi finals of the competition in 1956/57 season when they met the Busby Babes, although losing the first leg at the Dell 2-5, they battled gamely at Old Trafford. At one stage they were leading 3-1 on the night before finally winning 3-2 meaning United had won 5-7 on aggregate.

In 1979 Saints again reached the semis but found themselves without prolific scorer Steve Moran and they were knocked out by eventual winners Manchester City, In 2000 Saints faced Coventry City at the same stage and looked to have done the hard bit in gaining a 1-1 draw at Highfield Road, however after conceding a 2nd minute goal at The Dell, Saints couldn't find enough and went out 1-2 on aggregate.

After reaching the Final in 2005, Saints found themselves facing Liverpool in the 2006 semi. After losing 1-2 at Anfield and conceding an early goal in the second leg at St Mary's, Saints looked to be out before a last minute goal deadlocked the tie at 3-3 on aggregate. A goal apiece in the extra period meant penalties and Saints suffered heartbreak and were not to take part in their second final in two years.

Youngest player
Theo Walcott - 16 years, 143 days. v. Wolverhampton Wanderers. 6 August 2005.
Sadly within five months, after making only 13 appearances (10 as a substitute) scoring 5 goals, Walcott was sold to Arsenal for a fee that could rise to £12 million depending on appearances.

Young Men's Association
The foundations of Southampton Football Club were built when a curate of St Mary's Church convened a meeting of the young men of the parish to talk about football.

The meeting was held in the schoolrooms in Grove

Street just behind the Church itself, a short distance from the club's current home, St Mary's Stadium. The first item on the agenda of the newly formed Young Men's Christian Association was what type of football they would play – Rugby Football or the Association version. A long discussion took place and in the end it had to be put to the vote. Luckily for future generations, soccer was chosen.

The Young Men's Association of 1888, proud winners of the Junior Cup, and (below) a report of the team's very first match

So the newly titled Southampton St Mary's Young Men's Association played their first match on 21st November 1885 against Freemantle in Northlands Road. The Reverend A.B. Sole was the first President with Mr C. Abbott the first secretary and Mr A.A. Fry elected the team captain.

Within three years the football club appears to have dropped the title YMA, to be known simply as Southampton St Mary's. They maintained this title and presumably some link with the Church until 1897, when as it became clear that football was now a very serious business. St Mary's was dropped from the title and a limited company formed. The official title was Southampton Football and Athletic Company Limited, but to most and the world at large they would merely be Southampton Football Club

ST. MARY'S Y.M.C.A. v. FREEMANTLE ASSOCIATION FOOTBALL CLUB.—The football club which has just been formed in connection with St. Mary's Young Men's Asso-ciation, played their first match on Saturday last according to "Association Rules," when they showed that they have among their members the materials with which to form a fairly strong club by practice. During the first half St. Mary's scored four goals rather quickly, three of these being obtained from corner kicks. The game became much faster during the second half, and shortly after the change St. Mary's scored another point. Freemantle then obtained a goal through the ball from a corner kick passing off one of the St. Mary's team and so through the posts. Up to the call of time no further point was scored, so that St. Mary's were the victors by five goals to one. The goals were obtained by Bromley (three) and Fry (2). The Free-mantle team showed some good play during the latter part of the game, while the good individual play of each of the St. Mary's team was well sustained throughout.

Z
Zenith Data Systems Cup
An ironic name for a competition that saw Saints reach their zenith under Ian Branfoot, playing in the final of the last ever season of this competition. It had run for several years under several guises including The Full members Cup & The Simod Cup. Saints played the last game in the competition losing 2-3 to Nottingham Forest that presumably saw the east midlanders keep the Trophy.

HANDS UP FOR
THE PINK

FIRST FOR ALL YOUR LOCAL SPORTING ACTION

www.dailyecho.co.uk

Daily Ech